A RESILIENT *Life*

Bronwyn Jane
Christine Innes
Kleo Merrick
Lisa Ohtaras

Steph Gobraiel
Tracey Chapman
Vallye Adams

The Corporate Escapists

Copyright © 2023 by Christine Innes

All rights reserved. No part of this book may be reproduced in any form on or by an electronic or mechanical means, including information storage and retrieval systems, without permission in writing from the publisher, except by a reviewer who may quote brief passages in a review.

This book is designed to provide information and inspiration to our readers. It is sold with the understanding that the publisher is not engaged to render any professional advice. The content of each month is the sole expression and opinion of its author and not necessarily that of the publisher. No warranties or guarantees are expressed or implied by the publishers' choice to include any of the content in this book. Neither the publisher nor the author(s) shall be liable for any physical, psychological, emotional, financial, or commercial damages including, but not limited to, special, incidental, consequential or other damages.

First printed 2023 by The Corporate Escapists.

Printed on-demand in Australia, United States and the United Kingdom.

Table of Contents

Introduction   v

Christine Innes   2
The Journey to Resilience

Bronwyn Jane   20
Resilience Under Fire

Tracey Chapman   34
Rise Above With Resilience

Vallye Adams   50
The Power of Resilience

Lisa Ohtaras   66
The Gift of Bouncing Forward

Steph Gobraiel   80
The manual to business and motherhood called Life

Kleo Merrick   90
Resilient Entrepreneurship

Introduction

Welcome to A Resilient Life. As you embark on this transformative journey, you are about to encounter a collection of narratives that transcend borders and cultures, woven together by the indomitable spirit of resilience. This book is not just a compilation of stories; it's a guide, an exploration of the human capacity to not only endure adversity but to thrive in its wake.

In the pages that follow, you will meet remarkable women from different corners of the world, each contributing a unique thread to the rich tapestry of resilience. Their stories serve as beacons of strength, illuminating the path of bouncing forward after facing life's challenges.

Resilience is not a one-size-fits-all concept; it manifests in countless forms. You'll discover stories of leaving behind societal expectations, of entrepreneurial journeys marked by both triumphs and tribulations, and the unwavering commitment to a higher purpose. The essence of resilience is not merely bouncing back but bouncing forward, using adversity as a catalyst for growth.

As you delve into these narratives, consider this not just a book but a conversation—an invitation to explore your own resilience, to reflect on your journey, and to be inspired by the triumphs of others. The women you'll meet here— Lisa, Kleo, Tracey, Bronwyn, Vallye and Steph, —are not distant figures but companions on your own path. Their stories will echo in your own experiences, fostering a sense of connection and shared humanity.

So, turn the pages with an open heart. Let the collective wisdom within these stories be your guide as you navigate the complexities of life. May you find inspiration, practical insights, and, above all, the courage to embrace your own journey of bouncing forward.

Are you ready to embark on a transformative adventure? Let's begin.

Love and light

x Christine

CHAPTER 1

The Journey to Resilience

Unveiling the True Self, Navigating Entrepreneurship, and Overcoming Obstacles

"DREAMS + ACTION = REALITY"
~ Christine Innes

To all those on a life journey, use your story to fuel your passion and remember you are not defined by your past, create the brightest future for YOURSELF.

Christine Innes

Unveiling the True Self

Leaving the Corporate World: The Quest for Authenticity

Leaving behind the comfort and predictability of the corporate world can be a daunting decision. Many individuals embark on this journey in pursuit of something more profound: self-discovery and authenticity. The first step towards resilience often begins with a radical shift in identity. This shift occurs as individuals break away from societal norms and expectations, redefining themselves on their own terms.

In the corporate world, conformity is often celebrated, and employees may feel pressured to mold themselves into predetermined roles. This conformity can stifle personal growth and hinder one's ability to respond effectively to challenges. By stepping away from this environment, people have the opportunity to uncover their true selves.

Identity Transformation: A Personal Revolution

The journey of self-discovery is often marked by profound realisations. As individuals detach themselves from the corporate identity, they begin to confront questions about their passions, values, and authentic aspirations. This internal dialogue paves the way for a transformative experience that redefines their sense of self.

For many, this transformation is liberating. It provides a sense of clarity and purpose that can be a wellspring of resilience in the face of adversity. When individuals are no longer bound by societal expectations, they have the freedom to explore uncharted territories and develop a more profound understanding of themselves.

A RESILIENT *Life*

The Resilience of Self-Discovery

After my own not-so-gracious exit from corporate, the identify of not only who I was but also what I wanted to be was key in the first step to the transformation.

Learning to let go of what I thought society had planned for me and now following a path less travelled. The moment of realisation hit when I was asked what I am doing now after not seeing family and friends for over 10 years. Not one to be lost for words, this moment was "the moment' that had the ripple effect of changing my life.

It made me realise I did not know myself only a job title. I did not know what my passion, my purpose or even my own values where. It was time to figure it out.

Navigating Entrepreneurship

The Entrepreneurial Journey: A Leap into the Unknown

Once an individual has undergone the process of self-discovery and identity transformation, the next step often involves entrepreneurship. This journey can be exhilarating, but it is also fraught with uncertainties and challenges. Starting a business requires resilience, as entrepreneurs navigate uncharted territory.

The synergy between self-discovery and entrepreneurship is powerful. When individuals are aligned with their true passions and values, they are more likely to succeed in their entrepreneurial ventures. Their authenticity becomes a driving force, inspiring them to take risks and overcome obstacles.

Christine Innes

Discovering True Purpose: Igniting Entrepreneurial Spirit

The transition from a corporate career to entrepreneurship is often accompanied by a profound sense of purpose. This was certainly the case for me. After spending the the past few years, learning about myself, growing and healing, I started sharing my own story.

The reason was that when I was going through all of my life ups and downs, I felt alone, isolated, ashamed and riddle with guilt. I wanted to be a beacon of light for other so they did not feel any of this. That they are loved, they are heard, they are valued and not alone.

Resilience in the Face of Entrepreneurial Challenges

Stepping into owning my story was definitely, hard, and made me realise that with all of the obstacles I had faced, I am resilient and starting a business, I did have what it takes.

Most people focus on the business plan, the products, the services, I did it backwards, I started with myself to make sure I would be successful in my own mindset, and life in order to carry with the business. The business was personal, it was my story that starte it all, so if I wasn't in the right mindset, the business would not be as successful as it is today.

Overcoming Obstacles

When Business Slows Down: The Test of Resilience

No entrepreneurial journey is without its share of tough times. Every business faces periods of slow growth or adversity. Resilience is the force that keeps entrepreneurs going during these challenging phases.

A RESILIENT *Life*

Financial Challenges: Weathering the Storm

Financial difficulties are a common obstacle in entrepreneurship. Slow business growth or unexpected expenses can put a strain on an entrepreneur's resources. Resilience involves financial planning and the ability to adapt to changing circumstances. It also means being open to seeking assistance or guidance when needed.

Emotional Resilience: Staying Committed to the Mission

Entrepreneurs are emotionally invested in their ventures, making them susceptible to stress and burnout. Resilience in this context means maintaining a strong commitment to the mission and vision of the business. Sharing stories and experiences with like-minded individuals can be a source of emotional support and encouragement.

Operational Challenges: Adapting and Innovating

Operational challenges can arise at any stage of a business. Resilience entails the ability to adapt to changing market conditions, technologies, and consumer preferences. Entrepreneurs who continuously seek innovative solutions and remain agile in their operations are more likely to thrive.

Continuing the Mission: Inspiring Others

Resilience is not just about persevering through tough times; it is also about staying true to the mission of helping others find and follow their passions. Entrepreneurs who are unwavering in their commitment to this mission often inspire others to do the same.

In conclusion, the journey to resilience is a path of self-discovery, entrepreneurship, and overcoming obstacles. It is a transformative process where individuals break free from societal norms to become their authentic selves. Navigating the world of entrepreneurship, with its inherent uncertainties, becomes an extension of this journey. Resilience is the driving force that keeps entrepreneurs committed to their mission, even when business slows down. It is a testament to the human spirit's capacity to adapt, learn, and inspire others.

I can raise my hand and say I have encountered all of this over the past 4 years of business. Going out and getting a casual job to keep the finances in flow, to asking for help of others to get the business name out there, to even asking family members for financial support.

I truly believe that if my mindset was not resilient I would of closed the doors of the business.

The Breakthrough: Triumph of Resilience

The breakthrough, in the context of resilience, is the moment when individuals, after enduring numerous challenges and setbacks, experience a significant turning point in their journey. This breakthrough represents the culmination of their determination, perseverance, and unwavering commitment to their authentic selves and entrepreneurial aspirations.

The Epiphany: A Moment of Clarity

The breakthrough moment is often marked by a profound epiphany. It's the instant when individuals realize that their struggles and persistence were not in vain. This realization typically stems from a shift in perspective, a new strategy, or a combination of both. It's a moment of clarity where they see a clearer path forward.

For instance, when I left corporate, I wanted to leave all of the corporate world behind me. However, now I see that all the roles I have in my 22 years in corporate, lead me to be a leader, to know the systems and processes, the customer service and most of all the adapt.

Adaptability and Innovation: Key Drivers of Breakthroughs

Adaptability and innovation often play pivotal roles in achieving breakthroughs. Entrepreneurs who are resilient continually assess their strategies and adapt to changing circumstances. They embrace innovation to find creative solutions to ongoing challenges.

When Covid hit I was just about to launch the first issue of The Corporate Escapists Magazine. I could of crumbled and let it go as the world was closing down and who needed another magazine.

3 years later and when other magazines are shutting down, we are expanding. Being able to adapt and also be innovative in the way stories are delivered, in creating a community of story tellers, business owners and others needed that lighthouse to guide them is what made the magazine successful.

Overcoming Self-Doubt: The Personal Aspect of Breakthroughs

Resilience is not only about overcoming external challenges but also about conquering self-doubt and internal obstacles. Breakthroughs often involve a profound sense of self-belief and confidence. Entrepreneurs learn to trust in their abilities and the choices they've made.

For myself not letting the self-doubt the negative Nancy's in my life hold me back. I was taking a path least traveled and I needed to continue to back myself to show up for me. This is the the real resilience in all entrepreneurs.

Inspiration and Impact: The Resilience Ripple Effect

The beauty of breakthroughs is that they often have a ripple effect. Entrepreneurs who experience breakthroughs inspire others to follow their path. They become beacons of hope and resilience, demonstrating that with unwavering commitment and resilience, one can achieve their goals and make a meaningful impact.

Knowing that stories have a ripple effect this is what kept me going. Showing up and sharing my story to inspire others and create the impact that was needed in the world.

What is your ripple effect and how are you going to show up?

Celebrating Breakthroughs: Acknowledging the Journey

Breakthroughs are cause for celebration. They represent the culmination of a journey marked by hard work, determination, and the ability to face adversity head-on. It's essential to acknowledge and appreciate these moments of triumph.

Entrepreneurs who experience breakthroughs should take the time to reflect on their journey and celebrate their resilience. This reflection helps build inner strength, reinforces self-belief, and prepares them for future challenges.

A RESILIENT *Life*

In essence, the breakthrough is the pinnacle of resilience—a testament to the strength of the human spirit when aligned with authenticity and a higher purpose. It's a reminder that, even in the face of seemingly insurmountable challenges, individuals can achieve their goals and inspire others to do the same. The journey to resilience is transformative, and the breakthrough serves as a beacon of hope for all those who dare to pursue their passions and embrace their authentic selves.

Bouncing Forward: The Three Key Steps to Resilience

Bouncing forward is the ultimate goal of resilience. It goes beyond merely bouncing back from adversity; it involves using challenges as a catalyst for growth and transformation. To achieve this, individuals must take deliberate steps that foster personal and professional development.

Step 1: Acceptance and Adaptation

Resilience begins with acceptance. The first key step in bouncing forward is acknowledging the challenges and adversities faced. Denial or avoidance of problems can hinder progress. Instead, embracing the reality of the situation provides a solid foundation for resilience.

As someone who has avoidance issues, I found that the you need to face it head on. When the business wasn't growing and meeting the financial targets, I went and got a casual job. It was a quick fix, and yet it also gave me the drive to continue with the business as I knew that the business is helping others. For me to the be leader, it is leading with example. Leaving corporate and starting a business doesn't not mean you will not have challenges along the way, it si how you face these challenges, accept them and adapt to them.

I could of easily closed the business down and gave up, yet the drive in me, the resilience in myself and knowing the purpose of my business gave me the boost I needed.

Adaptation is the natural progression from acceptance. Resilient individuals are quick to adapt to changing circumstances. They are open to trying new approaches and strategies.

Step 2: Continuous Learning and Growth

Resilience is a journey of continuous learning and growth. Entrepreneurs who are committed to bouncing forward understand the importance of building on past experiences and mistakes. They view failures as opportunities for improvement.

I also say to my clients that starting a business will be the biggest personal development course you will ever do. When in corporate you are generally surrounded by a team, and you can focus on your role. Being in business you are the all the role - the accounts, the marketing, the sales, the promoter, the IT guru just to name a few. With each lesson learned in business, it is continuous business and personal growth you develop to help guide your business to the next level.

Step 3: Building a Support Network

Bouncing forward requires a robust support network. Resilient individuals understand that they don't have to navigate challenges alone. They seek support from mentors, advisors, peers, and their community.

Your tribe affects your vibe. If you do not have the right support network around you , it can be difficult to overcome the challenges. Most of my family have never had a business of their own, so when sharing challenges, it is easy for them to say ' just walk away it gave it a go'. Yet when sharing the challenges with my business minded friends, they give you ideas to think outside the box, plus also let you know you are not alone and 99% of them have encountered something similar. Find your tribe that will have raise your vibe and support you.

Conclusion: Bouncing Forward as the Ultimate Resilience

Bouncing forward is the culmination of the resilience journey. It involves acceptance, adaptation, continuous learning, growth, and building a strong support network. Those who embrace these steps are not only capable of weathering adversity but also of using it as a springboard for personal and professional development.

The journey of resilience is transformative and empowering. It allows individuals to break free from societal expectations, pursue their passions, and navigate the uncertainties of entrepreneurship. Along the way, they may encounter breakthroughs that propel them towards success and inspire others. Ultimately, bouncing forward is the ultimate testament to the human spirit's ability to not only endure but thrive in the face of adversity, continuing the mission to help people find and follow their passions.

I use the words bouncing forward as I believe that with every conversation, event, and moment in life we grow. We are never the same person afterwards. We do not go backwards we bounce forwards. Stepping into a new, brighter, more aware, more enlightened version of ourselves.

With every moment in your life, that you are called to show resilience remember you are bouncing forward to the life you are creating.

A Parting Gift: Embracing the Resilience Journey

As we conclude this exploration of resilience, I offer you a parting gift, one that encompasses the essence of bouncing forward in the face of life's challenges. Resilience is not a static state but a dynamic journey, and it is a gift that you can continually give to yourself. It's a gift that keeps on giving, fostering growth and personal development with every event, every moment.

Resilience is a Call to Action

Embracing resilience is an active call to action. It's a reminder that you are not merely a passive observer of your life's events but an active participant in shaping your destiny. Every challenge, setback, and opportunity is an invitation to practice resilience.

Think of it as a book that you continually write, one page at a time. The story of resilience is not about being immune to adversity but about mastering the art of responding to it. Each chapter in this book is a life event, a moment of growth, and a lesson learned. Your journey is unique, and your book of resilience is a testament to your strength and adaptability.

Learning from Free Resources: Your Personal Resilience Library

To embrace the journey of resilience, it's essential to be an eager learner. Resilience is a skill that can be honed, refined, and strengthened over time. It's a lifelong process of growth and self-discovery. Fortunately, there are abundant free resources available that can guide you on this journey.

Books, articles, podcasts, and online courses provide valuable insights into the art of resilience. They offer practical strategies,

A RESILIENT *Life*

inspirational stories, and expert advice to help you navigate life's challenges. Take the time to explore these resources, as they are like chapters in your personal resilience library. Each resource you engage with adds depth and nuance to your understanding of resilience, empowering you to face adversity with confidence.

Starting to Bounce Forward: A Commitment to Growth

Bouncing forward begins with a commitment to growth. It is a pledge to yourself that, regardless of the circumstances you encounter, you will use them as stepping stones toward personal and professional development. With every event, every moment, you have the opportunity to bounce forward.

Consider each moment of adversity as a teacher, offering valuable lessons. Embrace these experiences as opportunities to become a more resilient, empathetic, and adaptable individual. Whether it's a setback in your entrepreneurial journey, a personal challenge, or a societal crisis, you can choose to learn, adapt, and grow.

Resilience as a Gift to Share

One of the most beautiful aspects of resilience is that it's a gift you can share with others. Just as you have been inspired by the stories and experiences of resilient individuals, your journey can become an inspiration to those around you. By demonstrating resilience, you have the power to ignite the conversation about passion, authenticity, and unwavering commitment to a higher purpose.

When you bounce forward, you become a beacon of hope and an example of what is possible. Your journey, your breakthroughs, and your unwavering dedication to your mission can inspire others to embark on their resilience journey. It can encourage them to overcome their doubts and fears, follow their passions, and make a meaningful impact.

Conclusion: The Gift That Keeps on Giving

In closing, I offer you this parting gift: resilience. It is a gift that keeps on giving, a book that you continually write, and a journey that empowers you to bounce forward with every event and every moment. The call to action is yours, and the resources to learn and grow are abundant. It's a commitment to personal and professional development, and it's a gift you can share with the world.

As you embrace resilience, you are not only shaping your own destiny but also inspiring others to do the same. The journey is transformative, and the gift of resilience is a legacy that continues to flourish. So, as you face the challenges of life, may you bounce forward with resilience, passion, and a dedication to your mission of helping people find and follow their true passions.

x Christine

Christine Innes

The Corporate Escapists

Christine Innes is a visionary entrepreneur, storyteller, and the CEO and founder of The Corporate Escapists, a renowned media company that harnesses the power of storytelling to help entrepreneurs attract their ideal clients. With a deep understanding of the profound impact stories have on human connection and consumer behavior, Christine has revolutionized the way entrepreneurs communicate and sell their products and services.

After her own not so gracious exit from the corporate world, Christine shared her own personal story and realised she had a natural gift for storytelling. Fascinated by the captivating narratives that shaped cultures and societies, she realized that stories held the key to building strong connections and influencing people's perspectives. Armed with this knowledge, Christine embarked on a mission to create a platform that would empower entrepreneurs to leverage the power of storytelling to effectively sell their ideas and offerings.

In founding The Corporate Escapists, Christine recognized that stories have the unique ability to create emotional resonance and forge deep connections with audiences. She firmly believes that "stories sell, and facts tell." Drawing on her personal experience, Christine developed innovative strategies and frameworks that allow entrepreneurs to share their authentic stories, connect with their target audience, and ultimately attract their ideal clients.

Through The Corporate Escapists, Christine provides entrepreneurs with a platform to share their stories and amplify their voices. She understands that in a crowded marketplace, standing out and building trust is essential. By helping entrepreneurs craft compelling narratives and develop their personal brand, Christine enables them to differentiate themselves and forge meaningful connections with their ideal clients.

Under Christine's leadership, The Corporate Escapists has become a trusted resource for entrepreneurs seeking to communicate their brand stories effectively. Through coaching, workshops, and the production of high-quality multimedia content, Christine empowers entrepreneurs to tap into the transformative power of storytelling to grow their businesses and make a lasting impact.

In addition to her work with The Corporate Escapists, Christine is a sought-after speaker and thought leader in the field of storytelling and entrepreneurship. Her insights and strategies have helped countless individuals break through the noise, build authentic connections, and achieve remarkable success in their respective industries.

Outside of her professional endeavors, Christine is committed to giving back to society. She actively supports causes that promote education, empowerment, and creativity. Her belief in the power of stories extends beyond the realm of business, as she recognizes their ability to inspire change and foster a more compassionate world.

Christine Innes continues to drive innovation in the entrepreneurial landscape, empowering individuals to share their authentic stories, attract their ideal clients, and build thriving businesses. Her unwavering passion for storytelling, coupled with her expertise in marketing and business, make her a trailblazer in the industry, inspiring entrepreneurs worldwide to harness the power of stories to transform their lives and make a lasting impact

Facebook: @thecorporateescapists
Instagram: @thecorporateescapists
Email: hello@thecorporateescapists.com
Website: www.thecorporateescapists.com
YouTube: www.youtube.com/thecorporateescapists
Podcast: The Corporate Escapists Podcast

CHAPTER 2

Bronwyn Jane

Resilience Under Fire

Unleashing Your Unyielding Power and Living Authentically

"Be all you can be" ~ Bronwyn Jane

To Damien, my partner. Your unwavering commitment has transformed the challenges we faced into opportunities for growth and resilience. Together, we have weathered storms and celebrated victories, and I am endlessly thankful for the unwavering support you have provided. My journey is a testament to the power of love, understanding, and dedication. It is a reflection of the extraordinary bond we share, one that has transcended the ordinary and ventured into the realms of the extraordinary. Thank you for being my rock, my love, and my constant source of encouragement.

Bronwyn Jane

Beneath the surface

After a decade of dedicating my life to the banking world, I found myself at a crossroads in the form of a company merger, a sign that change was on the horizon. Despite my success and love of my job, I sensed it was time for something new. With a tinge of excitement and a bit of trepidation, I embarked on a journey to a different company, believing it would be a fresh start, an opportunity to continue using my financial expertise.

Little did I know, this move would hurl me into one of the most challenging periods of my life. The new company was undergoing its own transformations, and a wave of new faces was flooding in. On the surface, it sounded invigorating, but beneath the surface lay a storm I was unprepared for.

You see, my past had taught me resilience. I had grown up in a rural community where I was different, where I stood out for reasons I couldn't control. I was a bigger girl, not athletic, who couldn't read or spell, and terribly shy. My uniqueness became a magnet for bullies who found pleasure in tormenting me. Whether it was my lunch, my size, or my early physical development, I had faced ridicule before.

High school also had its challenges. Starting with boarding school and then moving to two different public schools, but nothing could compare to the onslaught of workplace bullying I faced in the future. The new company I had joined, with its promise of a fresh start, turned out to be a battlefield of cruelty. I encountered a level of bullying that cut deeper than anything I had experienced before.

On reflection, it's apparent life has a way of coming full circle, I suppose. In the professional world, just as in the schoolyard, there are challenges and lessons to be learned. This was a period that would test not just my resilience but also my capacity for growth. Leading me to unlock who I truly am and along the way revealing even in the face of adversity, we can find our strength and emerge wiser and stronger than before.

Crossroads of change

Growing up on a farm in the heart of the countryside, I learned life's most valuable lessons from the land itself. It was there with the unpredictability of nature, that my family instilled in me a set of core values that would shape me forever.

Respect was paramount in our household. Respect for our elders, respect for the land, and respect for the hard work that defined our lives. Doing as you were told was not just a rule; it was a way of life as it often keeps us safe. And when the day's work began, it didn't end until every task was completed. As the eldest, I bore responsibility that taught me the meaning of diligence and perseverance.

Resilience was not just a trait; it was a necessity etched into the very fabric of our existence. Living on the land meant facing the harsh realities of droughts, plagues, floods and poverty. Nature's whims were beyond our control, and we had to adapt. There were no quick fixes or easy solutions. If something broke, there were no professionals to call. We became our own plumbers, electricians, and mechanics. This ability to confront challenges head-on was the legacy of my family. They showed me, through their unwavering determination, that giving up was never an option.

When I ventured beyond the farm, the lessons of my upbringing became my guiding light. At the age of 18, I found myself in Sydney, a country kid navigating the complexities of life in a bustling city. Isolated and alone facing hardships that would have discouraged many, but I refused to be defeated. My home was two rooms in a run-down boarding house shared with questionable characters, cockroaches as roommates, a mattress and carpet with stains I dare not consider, and barely enough money to feed myself but I persevered. Meeting my challenges headlong, with the same tenacity I'd learned as a child.

At 21, I landed my dream job in a bank as a bank teller. For a decade, I thrived, climbing the corporate ladder until I became the youngest female senior manager. But then, life as I knew changed. The bank was sold, and a merger loomed. It was then that I decided to embrace change once more.

Moving to a new company seemed like a promising opportunity. The prospect of utilizing my talents in a new environment was enticing. Little did I know that this transition would thrust me into one of the most challenging periods of my life.

In the face of life's trials, I stood tall, drawing on the indomitable spirit instilled in me. The challenges only served to reinforce what I had always known: I was made of grit.

Beyond the abyss

It was the longest year and a half of my life. Every morning as I drove to my new job, dread settled in the pit of my stomach. The closer I got to the office, the tighter my chest became. I could barely breathe as I felt the tension building, my fingers involuntarily pulled my hair out as it wrapped around them. As I reached for the office door handle, I whispered to myself, hoping against hope, "I hope he's not here yet. I hope he's on the phone. Just let me get to my desk without him seeing me. Please, just give me that."

Once inside, I'd keep my head down, eyes fixed on my feet, avoiding any eye contact, and make a beeline for my desk. But it was futile. I knew what would follow. The moment I was spotted, the tirade would begin.

I was trapped in a workplace nightmare, enduring a boss unlike any I'd ever encountered before. He was a bully, a relentless tormentor who seemed to derive satisfaction from making my life unbearable. His anger, his frustration, he vented it all on me. Every single day, without fail. He screamed, he swore, he belittled me. I was denied the ability to do even the simplest tasks without his permission. And if I dare to do so the blitz of intimidation would begin. He thrived on control. It was a stark contrast to any previous experience I had encountered or even witnessed.

His onslaughts were relentless, ranging from the mundane to more personal attacks, questioning my competence and worth. I'd sit there, trembling, wondering why he chose me as the target for his anger. I had tried to speak up once but I quickly learned this only made things worse. I learned to shut up and take it.

Was this how he treated his family at home? Did they bear the brunt of his fury too? Or was it just a privilege saved for me?

The situation reached a breaking point when I discovered I was pregnant. This was a momentous event as doctors had said it wasn't possible. Screaming and abuse continued during the pregnancy. He was ruthless, taking me to the depths of despair where I couldn't see a way forward. Then I developed preeclampsia which could not be managed with any amount of medication. Doctors insisted I give birth a month early by emergency surgery to avoid a stroke or harm to my unborn child. My boss begrudgingly allowed me three weeks off, insisting I work from home as soon as I was out of the hospital. The screaming continued, albeit now over the phone.

When I returned to the office, he handed me an envelope. It was a cheque to make me go away, a subtle way of saying I didn't belong here. He cited my motherhood as a reason, claiming it didn't align with his vision of the role. It was a bittersweet moment as I was free from his tyranny, but I was left wondering about my future.

In the aftermath, as a young mother I pieced my life back together, I was left with invisible scars. But amidst the pain, I found my strength. I realized I was worthy of respect, of kindness, and that my voice mattered. I vowed never to allow myself to be subjected to such torment again.

Through the healing process, I became acutely aware of how people spoke to one another. Words became my refuge, my sanctuary. I made a promise to myself. I would rise above this experience, and I would help others do the same. The trauma had left its mark, but it hadn't broken me. I emerged stronger, more resilient, and armed with the knowledge that I deserved more.

I became my own advocate and embraced my worth, my strength, and my resilience. The road to healing was long, but I navigated it with determination and refusing to let the past define me. In the end, I emerged not as a victim but as a testament to the power of the human spirit to overcome even the darkest of times.

A RESILIENT *Life*

A voyage to self-respect

During the healing process a vow was etched into my soul that I would never allow anyone to treat me like that again. The profound lesson I learned during those dark days was clear. Tolerating someone's behaviour is akin to accepting it. It's a harsh truth that has become my guiding principle, urging me to reassess all experiences and relationships.

I had suffered in silence, cloaked in the belief that enduring silently was a mark of strength. However, I came to understand that true strength lies in sharing our struggles, our vulnerabilities, and our pain. It was a revelation. If we don't vocalize our battles, how can anyone extend a hand to help us navigate them? I learned the power of my voice, a tool that, when utilized, could summon guidance, support, and the unwavering presence of those who cared.

Through this transformative journey, I discovered the unyielding connection between my values and my boundaries. My values were not negotiable; they were the very essence of who I am, the core beliefs that shaped my identity. They became the pegs in the ground, marking the boundaries that safeguarded my integrity, self-respect, and well-being.

It's been a quest to define my boundaries, a task that proved to be as intricate as untangling a knotted ball of wool. Yet, as I navigated this process, I found clarity. My boundaries became steadfast, unmovable pillars in my life. As time went on people would challenge them, attempting to encroach upon my self-defined limits, but the difference now was my resolve. I stood firm, my boundaries bolstered by my newfound self-worth.

The gift of the experience has been the realization that no job, no amount of money, and no relationship could ever supersede the sanctity of my values and the boundaries that guarded them. My well-being is the epicenter of my existence, and I embraced the empowering truth that I deserve of a life that aligns with my principles, my beliefs, and my inherent worth.

The power of authenticity

The transformative odyssey from darkness to light led me down an unexpected path. A spiritual journey that began subtly but profoundly reshaped my very essence. Gently I delved deep into the core of my being, unraveling layers of my soul I hadn't known existed. Through the experiences that unfolded, I not only discovered my true self, but I also etched my values and boundaries into the very fabric of my soul. This integration birthed an unparalleled inner strength, a reservoir of power and resilience.

Connecting with this newfound version of me provides an overwhelming sense of daily peace. Stress and triggers became foreign concepts, replaced by an awareness that seemed to flow from a limitless source within. Those around me noticed the transformation, my friends and family recognized the grounded authenticity that now radiated from my very core.

Gone are the days of obliging nods and reluctant 'yeses.' Instead, my voice embeds the truth of my heart. Every word spoken is genuine, and in this authenticity, I discovered a source of empowerment. Fear is replaced by a sense of knowing, a knowledge that being true to oneself is an invincible shield. When you are authentic, nothing can pierce your armor, for you stand in your truth, unshaken by others.

Another profound lesson has been bestowed and that is the power of embracing every facet of my being, even the flaws and mistakes. By acknowledging them, I owned them. And when I do, the shackles that bind me are released. They become stepping stones, reminders of my humanity and my capacity to grow. When I shared my fears and my mistakes, they lost their hold on me. No longer could they be weaponized against me. Instead, they became threads in the tapestry of my authenticity, proof of my resilience and willingness to face life's challenges head-on.

The journey had taught me that true strength lay in vulnerability, in accepting every aspect of oneself, and in living authentically. In this newfound authenticity, there is liberation, and in that liberation, there is a peace that surpasses all expectations. The power of embracing my authentic self was not just a lesson; it was a revelation, a truth that had the potential to transform not only my life but also the lives of those I touched. It was a testament to the incredible strength that resides within each of us, waiting to be embraced.

A purpose-driven journey

Every day, I step into the world as my true self, a version of me I never thought I'd have the courage to embrace. I lead a life that's driven by purpose. Finally embracing who I am, as a psychic, medium, and spiritual coach, I've found my calling in transforming lives through deep connections and heightened awareness. My mission? To translate the intricate energy of the world into words, articulating what many feel but find hard to express. I guide others to do the same.

Embracing authenticity didn't just open doors; it unlocked an entirely new world. Through my commitment to being genuine, I founded the Psychic Mediumship College. Facing my mistakes and fears head-on allowed me to connect with some of the most influential people in my industry. Taking me across the world from Australia to America, where I was able to use my gifts with others.

In this transformative process lives change right before my eyes. There's no greater gift than knowing you've impacted someone's life positively. This experience has become my driving force, propelling me to follow my purpose.

Which is clear now, to show people how to live the life they've always dreamed of. Through authenticity, connection, and the power of embracing our true selves, I aim to inspire others to step into their own light. In doing so, I believe we can create a ripple effect of positivity, kindness, and empowerment that can touch every corner of the world.

Gratitude in growth

In the depths of my transformative journey, I stumbled upon invaluable lessons that reshaped my perspective on life, love, and self-worth. These profound revelations have become guiding stars, illuminating my path and inspiring others on their own journeys. Here are some of the most impactful learnings that I want to share:

1. What You Tolerate, You Receive.

The universe mirrors back to us what we allow in our lives. Tolerating negativity, disrespect, or mistreatment sets a precedent. By setting boundaries and refusing to tolerate anything less than respect, we invite positivity and love into our lives.

A RESILIENT *Life*

2. Facing Fears Diminishes Their Power.

Fear is a formidable force until we confront it. Facing our fears head-on robs them of their ability to control us. It's within this confrontation that we discover our inner strength and resilience.

3. Bravery in Authenticity and Vulnerability.

True bravery lies in being authentic and vulnerable. It takes courage to reveal our genuine selves, flaws and all. Embracing our vulnerabilities doesn't make us weak; it showcases our strength.

4. Unrecognized Resilience.

We often underestimate our own resilience. In the face of adversity, we discover depths of strength we didn't know existed. Our ability to bounce back from challenges showcases the extraordinary resilience inherent within each of us.

5. Self-Love Is Not Selfish.

Prioritizing self-love and self-care is an act of kindness to self, not selfishness. When we honour and love ourselves, we set a standard for how others should treat us. It's through this self-love that we teach the world how to value us.

6. Define Your Values.

Take the time to introspect and create a list of your core values. Are you honest, trustworthy, compassionate? Evaluate if your current actions align with these values. If not, embrace the power to change. Define the person you want to be, and let that vision guide your actions.

This wisdom isn't just theoretical. It's a roadmap for living a life that resonates with our authentic selves. By internalizing these lessons, we can navigate the complexities of life with grace and purpose, fostering meaningful connections and profound self-discovery along the way.

Shared with immense appreciation of your journey alongside mine.

Bronwyn Jane

Bronwyn Jane

Psychic Medium & Psychic Mediumship College

In the intricate tapestry of life, Bronwyn emerges as a rare and remarkable bridge between the tangible and the mystical. In 2017, she made a courageous leap, leaving behind the familiar confines of a thriving retail business to fully embrace her innate gifts as a psychic medium. Her journey, marked by this pivotal decision, represents a blend of audacity and dedication that has set her apart in the spiritual realm.

With a background steeped in the corporate world in banking and finance, Bronwyn's venture into the metaphysical was an extraordinary departure from her comfort zone. Despite her initial skepticism, she embarked on a profound quest to unlock the mysteries that had captivated her since childhood. Guided by revered mentors like Lisa Williams and Tony Stockwell, she delved deep into the realms of spirituality, investing over 15 years in intensive metaphysical training and practice.

Bronwyn's exceptional abilities have not only made her a sought-after psychic medium, conducting over 400 readings annually but have also earned her international recognition. Sharing the stage with legendary figures like Lisa Williams, she mesmerizes vast audiences with her platform mediumship. Beyond her role as a practitioner, Bronwyn is a Certified Master Teacher and founder of the Psychic Mediumship Collage, dedicating herself to shaping aspiring psychics and mediums into confident, ethical practitioners. Her approach is a harmonious fusion of extensive experience, natural talent, and exceptional training, culminating in a captivating stage presence that resonates deeply with audiences worldwide.

College Website: www.PsychicMediumshipCollege.com
Reading Website: www.BronwynJaneMedium.com
Email: info@bronwynjanemedium.com
Facebook: BronwynJaneMedium
Instagram: bronwynjanemedium
LinkedIn: bronwyn-jane-36209122b
TikTok: @bronwynjanemedium

Tracey Chapman

Author, Resilience & High Performance Coach. Australia.

CHAPTER 3

Tracey Chapman

Rise Above With Resilience

"Pain is not a place to live; lighting our soul up and living is!" ~ Tracey Chapman

To my son Tristan for honouring me to be your mother.

To my husband for always being by my side and giving me the love and support, especially on my darkest days.

To my son Shannon and my fur babies, thank you for showing me the true meaning of love and reminding me that life is beautiful.

Tracey Chapman

The farmer's daughter...

A little wet nose pulls me from my slumber. "Morning, Joey, come on, jump up in bed with me. It's freezing". Our pet kangaroo, who lives inside with us, loves to jump in bed and snuggle, especially on these freezing cold mornings.

I can hear the joyful sounds of my mum bustling about in the kitchen, and oh boy, the aroma of her baking fills the air! My mum is truly a culinary genius. She always has a comforting pot of soup simmering on our trusty wooden stove to keep us cozy during these chilly winter days.

Nothing brought me greater joy than spending time with my mum in the kitchen, lending a hand with our baking adventures. We were raised to appreciate homemade delicacies, rather than relying on store-bought cakes or meals. It was a special bond we shared and an invaluable lesson in the art of creating something from scratch. I inherited my mum's love of cooking.

I was fortunate to grow up as the youngest among five siblings, two elder sisters and two brothers. Our childhood revolved around the beautiful farm life, with acres of open spaces and the freedom to explore. We enjoyed the blessings of nature with homegrown fruits, vegetables, and meat straight from our farm.

Growing up, I was a young girl with a tomboyish spirit that couldn't be tamed. The sight of me in dresses was as rare as spotting a unicorn. Even today, as an adult, I find comfort and confidence in my trusty jeans or pants. But it wasn't just about my choice of clothing; it was about the adventures that awaited me beyond the confines of frilly skirts.

I vividly remember spending countless hours on our family farm, zooming around on our rugged motorbike. The wind

A RESILIENT *Life*

rushing through my hair, the thrill of exploration fueling my every move – those were the moments that truly defined me.

While other girls may have been content playing with dolls or at tea parties, I craved the exhilaration of discovering new territories and pushing boundaries. The farm became my playground, and the motorbike was my trusted steed.

From navigating bumpy trails to exploring hidden nooks and crannies, every ride brought a sense of liberation and empowerment. It was as if the open fields whispered secrets only meant for me to discover.

Sure, there were times when dirt smudges adorned my face instead of dainty makeup or when scrapes and bruises served as badges of honour rather than delicate scars. But those battle wounds only fueled my determination to conquer new challenges day after day.

In a world where societal expectations often dictate what is considered 'girly' or 'proper,' I proudly embraced my tomboyish nature. It taught me resilience, independence, and an unwavering belief in following my own path rather than conforming to stereotypes.

Embracing resilience...

Growing up as a farmer's daughter, I played an active role in supporting my family on the farm. My father always emphasised the importance of giving our very best. If something didn't work out initially, he taught me to keep trying until I succeeded. This valuable lesson instilled a tremendous resilience that has carried me through life's challenges.

Tracey Chapman

I grew up in Boyup Brook, a small town located in the southern region of Western Australia. Like many others in rural areas, I followed the traditional path of marrying at a young age.

After tying the knot, my partner and I made the decision to move from Boyup Brook to Collie with the intention of starting our own business. Shortly after settling into our new location, we were overjoyed to welcome our first child, Shannon. And just 20 months later, we were blessed with the arrival of our second child, Tristan.

Oh my goodness! Prepare to be amazed by these two absolutely adorable little boys, who could easily be mistaken for angels themselves! With their curly blond hair and precious cherub noses, they are the epitome of cuteness. And let's not forget those mesmerising eyes - Shannon with his enchanting brown eyes and Tristan with his captivating blue/grey eyes that seem to change with the light.

From the very beginning, I possessed a clear vision of what I wanted to achieve in my life. I understood that the key to living the life of my dreams rested solely in my own hands, regardless of being married.

To bring about the life I envisioned, I was determined to put in the necessary hard work and dedication. Above all, one of my biggest motivations was providing my sons with a future filled with endless opportunities and experiences that would surpass all expectations.

One moment can change everything...

Health and fitness were in my blood...We opened our own health club in Collie, and I would spend daylight hours teaching and working in the health club and nighttime hours packing shelves at Coles.

The long hours and getting as little as two to four hours of sleep a night for five to six nights a week took its toll. Being one of the top packers and youngest in the team, I was assigned the hardest aisle with the heaviest boxes to lift. I would get home in the early morning hours at around 4am and grab a shower and a few hours of sleep.

Tristan, at the tender age of three, would totter into the bathroom while I was showering, eager to give me a warm hug. "Mummy's home," he would say, before happily wandering back to his bed. It brought him such joy knowing that I was finally home.

When my two boys were just four and six years old, my marriage was going through a difficult time. As a result, I made the decision to start fresh and moved with the boys to Perth. It was a significant transition, but it marked the beginning of a new chapter as I embraced my role as a dedicated single mother raising two wonderful boys.

I climbed the corporate ladder and thrived in this world. I was providing the boys with the lifestyle I wanted them to have. The harder I worked, the better the income, and the more I could give them.

At the age of 21, Shannon made the bold decision to move to Melbourne and pursue a career as an Interior Designer. Three years later, at the age of 24, he took another leap of faith and relocated to Shanghai to further his professional journey.

Tristan's journey as a Youth Pastor began at the age of 17, fueled by his unwavering passion for helping children and young adults facing difficult circumstances. Whether they were struggling with drug addiction, experiencing abuse, or lacking a stable home life, Tristan was determined to make a positive impact and let them know they were valued.

From a young age, Tristan has been a transformative force, touching many lives and selflessly giving without expecting anything in return. He lived by the motto "Go Change The World" and always greeted the people in his community with a warm bear hug and heartfelt "I love you."

I was at home, working with a business partner. He had just left when my phone rang. It was Brisita, Tristan's fiancé. "I don't want to worry you, but I wanted to let you know that Tristan is missing. I've already called the police, and I'm not sure if you'd like to come over to Tristan's house."

"I'll be right over", I replied.

As I drove from my place on the freeway to Tristan's house, which was approximately a 40-minute drive, my mind and heart were racing. I felt a sickening sensation in my stomach, and a sudden wave of dread washed over me. Despite my urgency to find out where my son was, I made a conscious effort not to exceed the speed limit.

I called my husband, Paul, who was at a conference, to inform him about what had happened. Although he wanted to rush to Tristan's to meet me, I advised him to stay at the conference. "Stay at the conference. Everything will be alright," I assured him. I promised to keep him updated as soon as I had more information.

Upon arriving at Tristan's place, I was greeted by one of his work colleagues who kindly escorted me into his lounge. Shortly after, the police arrived and introduced themselves. Brisita, meanwhile, was being kept in another room.

A RESILIENT *Life*

I found myself being bombarded with a million questions, causing panic to rise within me. I struggled to comprehend the situation and provide answers, making it difficult to think straight.

The police left me alone while they went outside to take a call. Upon their return, the young police officer displayed genuine concern.

The next words I heard were, "I'm sorry, but your son has been found. He is deceased."

I could hear screaming, screams of a wild animal in pain. Those screams were mine!

My son had taken his own life.

My whole world had collapsed in that one day—that one phone call—that one moment.

In a moment of extreme panic and feeling completely isolated, the compassionate police officer offered me a lifeline by asking if there was someone I needed to reach out to. Without any second thoughts, I immediately dialed my husband's number, knowing that he would respond with urgency and come to my aid as swiftly as possible.

Tristan's loved ones were promptly informed through phone calls, ensuring that his father, brother, family, and friends were made aware of the situation. It was of utmost importance to keep them all informed and involved during this time.

As Tristan's mother, I was asked to identify his body. How? How can I possibly do this? How can I find the strength to get through this? My beautiful boy, who meant the world to me. I carried him in my womb and gave birth to this precious boy whom I loved with all my heart.

Tracey Chapman

The following days, weeks, and months spent working through funeral arrangements and police inquiries felt like the darkest of nightmares. It is a nightmare that no mother should ever have to endure.

I underwent a profound physical and emotional shutdown as I tried to deal with the excruciating pain that was deeply rooted within me. It felt as if my heart had been mercilessly ripped away, leaving me completely devastated.

During the night, I was tormented by unsettling nightmares, causing tears to flow down my face as I lay in bed. Unable to find solace in sleep and not wanting to wake my husband, I would wander aimlessly through the house, overwhelmed by a deep sense of despair for my dear boy.

Exhaustion consumed my days, leaving me with no will to push through.

I found myself becoming a mere shadow of who I once was, as a deep sense of emptiness consumed me from within.

Part of me died with my son.

The question of WHY, was too profound.

The torment of "Why did I not realise something was wrong?" "Why did he not call me?"

These questions were driving me insane.

The Constable, who was in charge of Tristan's case, told me that for a mother, the suicide of her child is one of the most challenging things to cope with, and many do not overcome it. She was not mistaken.

A RESILIENT *Life*

Pain is not a place to live...

As someone who has always relied on my strengths and resilience to cope in the past, I thought I was doing alright.

I've never been fond of photos taken of me. However, one day, as I glanced at a recent photo, I couldn't help but be struck by a thought: "Who is this person I see? She looks so sad." It was at that moment when I realised the absence of light in my eyes, replaced only by an overwhelming sadness.

It was at this very moment that I had to acknowledge that I was not alright.

I found myself consumed by deep sorrow and torment, and unfortunately, I was taking out this anguish on my husband and fur babies. It was a painful realisation that I couldn't continue to destroy my life with them, just as I was destroying myself.

I had to find a way to transcend my pain and embrace life once more.

I tapped into the depths of my resilience and strength, determined to recover and lift myself out of deep despair. I found the motivation to start living again, not only for my husband, Shannon, and my fur babies but also for my son, Tristan.

Tristan did not take my life. He took his own.

I got to work... My healing journey began

I utilised my research skills, honed from my background in the corporate world, to embark on a journey of self-discovery and healing after the devastating loss of my son.

I dedicatedly conducted thorough research on the top gurus in the fields of mindset, resilience, spirituality, and personal development. I fully immersed myself in their teachings, absorbing all the knowledge I could find.

I read book after book on trauma, grief, and recovery.

I attended mastermind after mastermind on spirituality, personal development and mindset.

Tony Robbins was one of my mentors, and I travelled to attend his Unleash the Power Within and Date With Destiny.

At Date With Destiny, held in Cairns, Queensland, the day that Tony talked about suicide, I felt that Tony was talking directly to me.

The pain that I had buried deep within, with the lid shut tight, started to bubble to the surface. As I allowed myself to feel the deep pain hidden in my soul, it raged through me.

It was the most painful experience during my journey of self-acceptance and breaking open. I was held tightly by my fellow team as every little emotion surfaced.

I tried therapy, but it only kept me in pain—a place I did not want to reside in.

I was eagerly absorbing every bit of knowledge that crossed my path. One day, while scrolling through my Facebook page, I came across an advertisement by Brendon Burchard about High-Performance Coaching. After investigating what the coaching was all about and speaking with one of his team members, I thought to myself, "I've tried everything else, so why not give this a shot?" With that mindset, I eagerly signed up to be coached by one of Brendon's top coaches.

A RESILIENT *Life*

My coach was truly amazing. During the time I worked with her, we developed a deep bond. With her guidance and thought-provoking questions, my healing transformation was truly profound.

I wholeheartedly embraced the task and faced my pain head-on, acknowledging that it was the only way to find true joy, happiness, and the ability to fully embrace life once again.

Thanks to my personal transformation with Brendon's style of High-Performance Coaching, I made the decision to attend his coaching program. I am proud to announce that I am now a Certified High-Performance Coach.

Being passionate about resilience, I have been studying it through PositivePsychology to further enhance my skills in this area.

Who are you going to become...

I wanted to make Tristan proud, knowing that his mum refused to give up the fight for her life.

Every card he gave me always had the most beautiful message. "I love your strength Mum and how you always get back up." "I love and admire you."

I cherish these cards and have them stored in a beautiful box.

We are not the same person on the other side of our loss. It is crucial for us to embrace the journey of self-discovery and uncover the person we are destined to become.

Everything we once valued, which seemed important, no longer carries the same weight.

I wholeheartedly embraced everything I had studied, which greatly aided my healing process and guided me towards creating a new identity for myself - my new ME. As a result, I have developed a program called "Rebuild Your Power Life," which is specifically designed to assist executives in rebuilding their lives with strength and purpose after experiencing a devastating loss.

This program will help you go beyond therapy, self-help, and support groups to finally break through grief, reignite your inner fire, and find a new life filled with meaning, impact, and purpose - in just eight quick weeks.

As a high-performer who's walked this journey of grief and recovery, and come out on the other side, I have the rare blend of experience and credentials to make a lasting difference in people's lives as a Resilience and Certified High Performance Coach.

For more information on my products, services, and free resources, please visit: www.traceyachapman.com

We have been given one life to live, and it is up to us to live our best life....

If I can empower you in any way through my journey, I would like to share some of my biggest learnings with you. I hope these insights can help you on your healing path forward.

1. Live for your loved ones! Though they may have lost their lives, you still have the opportunity to cherish yours. Honour their memory by embracing life to the fullest. Remember, they are always with you in spirit.

2. You possess a strength that surpasses your own perception! Take a moment to delve deep within yourself, and you will

A RESILIENT *Life*

discover your own extraordinary gifts, talents, and inner strength. Embrace these qualities and move forward with the love of your loved ones in your heart.

3. Find acceptance in your pain! Embrace it as part of your journey towards healing. It is through acceptance that the true healing process can begin.

4. Allow yourself to break open! Until you release that deep, dark pain, it will remain trapped within your body, impacting your health and overall well-being. Although it may be a painful step, it is incredibly worthwhile. Give yourself permission to cry, to scream, to get angry, and to truly feel your pain.

5. We don't simply move on from grief. Instead, we learn to live our lives while still carrying the weight of our grief.

6. Give yourself grace! Each of our paths to healing will be different. There is no direct pathway forward. It goes in twists and turns, ups and downs. Love yourself and find comfort on your journey.

"Embrace the gift of life by living it to the fullest and honouring every moment." ~ Tracey Chapman

From my heart to yours,

Tracey xxx

Tracey Chapman

Tracey A Chapman

Tracey Chapman is an Author, and Resilience and Certified High-Performance Coach.

Tracey is one of the few Resilience and Certified High-Performance coaches in the world who has walked the painful grief journey and now specialises in helping executive men and women find new passion, purpose, and meaning and rebuild their lives after a devastating loss.

Tracey's signature program "Rebuild Your Power Life", will help you go beyond therapy, self-help, and support groups to finally break through grief, reignite your inner fire, and find new life filled with meaning, impact, and purpose - in just eight quick weeks.

Tracey has been exclusively interviewed by Brainz Magazine for an article titled "Navigating Grief to Rediscover Power" and has graced the front cover of their August 31, 2023 issue.

Being a lover of Corgi's, Tracey has written several children's books, Queenie Is Taught Manners at The Corgi Ranch, about the importance of manners. Her books are for all parents with toddlers and toddlers who are strong-willed to teach their toddlers manners in a gentle, compassionate, and loving way.

Tracey is dedicated to fostering a movement "Thrive After Grief" where we can all thrive after experiencing grief. Our past does not define us, and we have the power to craft a new, empowering narrative that embraces our resilience and strength gained through our challenges. Let us rewrite our story, knowing that it will be even more powerful because of what we have overcome.

Website: www.traceyachapman.com
Email: info@traceyachapman.com
Facebook: traceyachapmanbiz
Instagram: traceyachapman
LinkedIn: traceychapman2

CHAPTER 4

Vallye Adams

The Power of Resilience

Unleashing the Extraordinary Within You

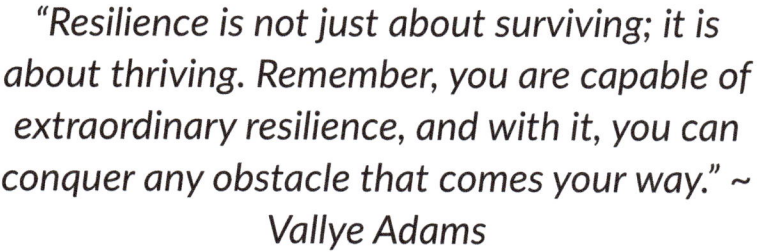

"Resilience is not just about surviving; it is about thriving. Remember, you are capable of extraordinary resilience, and with it, you can conquer any obstacle that comes your way." ~ Vallye Adams

> To my husband, Jason and my three most loved blessings, Christian, Vallye Catelynn and Makayla; you are my resiliency. For you, I will always strive to be a better person, a better mom and wife, a better example of strength, perseverance and resilience. Because of you, my resilience and love will last for eternity.

Vallye Adams

What is resilience??

In the face of all of life's challenges, resilience is the remarkable quality that empowers us to navigate the tough waters of adversity and emerge stronger than ever. It is the unwavering belief in our ability to overcome obstacles, the determination to persist and keep going, no matter what, in the face of setbacks. It is the courage and determination to rise above even the worst circumstances. Resilience is not merely about bouncing back, but rather, it is the ability and capacity to leap forward, to embrace a changed mindset, and to find a way to thrive in the face of adversity.

WOW! Well, how do we find resilience within ourselves?? Let's think about this: first, find a quiet, dimly lit space. Think back over your entire life. Close your eyes, take a deep breath, and really focus. Think about, recall a time(s) where you felt overwhelmed, exhausted, or truly disappointed. Maybe you were depressed, felt defeated, hurt to the core, or heartbroken. Was there a time when you were truly at your lowest, darkest time? Did all you want to do was hide under a rock, or pull your covers over your head and stay in bed forever? Maybe you felt unsure if you could even make it to the next day. If right now is NOT one of these times, then ask yourself, how did you get here today, right now?? If you are reading this chapter, how did you get yourself out of that rut and back to yourself? What empowered you to bounce forward to the positive, thriving, moving forward, brighter, and happier times you are in now?? Whatever you did, however you made that change or "leap forward", **that was and IS RESILIENCE!!!** In my chapter, I would like to explore the incredible power of resilience, how I have been able to use it and how you can also, to inspire and motivate yourself and others to unleash your extraordinary potential.

A RESILIENT *Life*

Understanding Resilience

I think it is very important to understand "Resilience" is not an innate trait; it is a skill that can be developed, honed, and mastered. If we understand its core components, we can better develop resilience in our lives and inspire others to do the same. If you don't have resilience "mastered", then how can we further develop and cultivate strong resilience??

MINDSET: Our mindset plays a pivotal role in developing resilience. Adopting a growth mindset, where challenges are viewed as opportunities, is a great first start. Perhaps changing, redesigning your thinking that our struggles and dark times are not so dark, but a time to focus on growth within ourselves. Have you ever thought to step away from the despair feeling and look deeper into what challenges you are facing. Can perhaps these setbacks be teaching us something about ourselves? Is there something we can do, think, or approach differently? I love the saying, "if you want something to change, you have to change something". Perhaps, a change of mindset can be the change in yourself.

For me, when things/times are rough, when I am feeling disheartened, like nothing is fair or going right, or experienced what I feel is a setback or "failure", after sulking for a while, I know (and remind myself) the only person who is going to get me out of my rut is ME. I tell myself, it is time for me to get out of my head and change my mindset. One of my "go-to's" is to play music, specifically selected, what I call "pump me up" music, that I know resets me and my mindset.

The song by Michael Jackson, "Man in the Mirror" is one of them. **"I'm starting with the man in the mirror, I'm asking** him to make a change … .if you wanna make the world a better place, take a look at yourself and then make a change."

Another one for me is, "It's My Life", by Bon Jovi. **"Tomorrow's getting harder, make no mistake. Luck ain't even lucky, got to make your own breaks. It's my life and it's now or never. Cause I ain't gonna live forever, I just wanna live while I'm alive."**

I have many "pump me up" songs that inspire and motivate me. An entire playlist to be honest. These songs help me to look at and feel things differently. I try to absorb the words, sounds, vibe and feeling of the music and focus on finding a different approach, a different mindset with whatever challenges I am facing. Personally, I have learned from some very difficult times, that life is so short and none of us are promised tomorrow. During challenging times and adversities, I channel and remember my mom, her life, love, and inspiration as well as the vibrant life, taken so young and too soon, of my young niece, Lilly. Songs are how I reflect, refocus, and reset myself. The music and words are how I redirect my mindset through tough times. I strive to find the lesson, the challenge, failure or setback is teaching me. Do you have a favorite song (or playlist) that inspires and motivates you?? Have you ever tried this approach during those dark times as you search for resilience?

By looking at our setbacks and tough times through a different window in our minds, this can help us adapt our thinking and feelings of despair. It can help us to see things more positively. By embracing a positive outlook, we can better focus on our resilience as we navigate life's inevitable ups and downs.

Of course, there is much more to resilience than just changing your mindset. Resilience thrives in the face of challenges. Yes, if we can adapt our mindset to look at obstacles more as an opportunity, we can harness their transformative power and inspire others to do the same. However, it is important to remember, resilience is not about avoiding obstacles, but about finding ways to overcome them.

How can we reframe setbacks as opportunities for growth and learning?? Each day, working on finding a positive attitude, seeking support when needed, and using problem-solving strategies. If we can do this, I believe we can overcome and see these obstacles, challenges, and adversities in a different light, thus emerging stronger than before.

Embracing challenges and failure

How do we embrace the challenges, adversities, and even failures?? Have you heard the inspirational saying, "There's no such thing as FAILURE. Either you WIN or you LEARN. Love this. Another way to develop your resilience is to embrace failure not as an end destination, rather a stepping stone towards success. Sounds a little odd to use failure and success in the same sentence, right?? But, by looking at something you have failed at, as NOT a failure, but valuable feedback and an opportunity to change, learn and grow, you can and will bounce back with a new sense of determination and resilience.

Do you have any "failures" in your lifetime? I do. There are many things I have "failed" at throughout my lifetime. So many. If I look back on my life, this entire chapter could be filled with hundreds of examples on what NOT to do and how many times I have failed myself, my family, my career, friends, family, and on and on. However, when people meet me, work with me, get to know me, or even google my name, they would never tell you or even think "wow, she sure has messed up!". But I have, I really have!!! Here's one example: never finishing college? In my mind, this is my biggest regret and to me, certainly a FAILURE on so many levels. Do I dwell on it, think about it daily, share it with everyone I meet, or let it define me? NO. I choose NOT to let my mindset or actions allow this to define me or my future. Although hard at times, I make the conscious effort to remind myself to see this as not a failure, rather an opportunity to keep growing and pushing forward. Whenever disappointment creeps in, I refocus my mindset to see that education is not limited to the confines of a classroom and that my life experiences are ultimately my greatest teacher. I focus my thinking to remember all the many accomplishments achieved and strive to keep building and growing. This helps me build my confidence and resilience, bouncing back stronger and stronger each time.

Others don't know about, see, or hear about my failures, because they are not something I chose to focus or dwell upon. My failures do not define me and yours do not define you. It's important to remember we are not perfect; everyone makes mistakes, and we all experience rough, dark times and setbacks.

Resilience requires us to be kind and compassionate towards ourselves. When we practice self-compassion, it helps us to embrace our imperfections, acknowledge our struggles, and treat ourselves with the same empathy and understanding we offer to others. Trying to give myself the compassion I offer others is certainly a challenge. However, adapting to give myself compassion, learn something (or many things) from my mistakes and during the rough times is a priority. If I am dwelling on, constantly talking about, or sharing failures or challenges, this is not possible.

This self-nurturing approach helps develop resilience and helps us bounce back from setbacks with greater strength. Always a work in progress for me although I focus on improving this approach always.

A RESILIENT *Life*

Adaptability and Finding Purpose and Meaning

Resilience requires adaptability—a willingness to embrace change and navigate uncharted territories. By cultivating adaptability, we become more flexible, open-minded, and resourceful, enabling us to face adversity with resilience and creativity. Every single day, although sometimes difficult, I give it my all to reset and focus my mindset, find the positive, learn from and adapt failures into a teaching moment and sometimes turn them into a win. My goal is to remind myself my setbacks and failures are a reminder to look in the mirror and "make that change" and find a way to make the difference I strive for. How have you adapted, changed, to find resilience? Does this come naturally or something you must work at??

Life is ever evolving, and learning to embrace change is crucial for personal and professional growth. Our ability to adapt and evolve allows us to thrive. The peak of resilience: not only adapting your mindset but having the opportunity to encourage others to also embrace change as an opportunity for self-discovery and personal growth.

Do you know your purpose? Your reason for living? Maybe your passion ignites in you, your reason for existing. Having a sense of purpose and meaning in life fuels our resilience. When we connect our actions to something greater than ourselves, we find the motivation and courage to persevere through challenging times. My purpose fuels me. It ignites in me the action of helping to make a difference for nonprofit organizations. I call it, "Helping the Helpers". I find that helping others makes a difference in the world, whether it's helping those with different abilities, feeding the hungry, research for disease, providing for those less fortunate, this reminds me of the things that are greater than myself. Being a part of change, helps fuel my ability to remain strong through my toughest times and remind myself to find and remain resilient.

Encouraging others to discover their purpose can ignite their resilience, helping them to overcome obstacles and thrive. I am proud my purpose in life is twofold; helping the helpers, fuels my resiliency, AND it encourages others to do the same. Resilience is not an individual pursuit; and it isn't just about helping myself develop it. By fostering resilience within ourselves and others, we create a ripple effect of strength and empowerment.

No one can do this alone

No one can navigate life's challenges alone. Surrounding yourself with a supportive network of friends, family, and mentors is essential for personal growth. By sharing your experiences, you encourage others to seek out positive relationships that provide encouragement, advice, and a helping hand during difficult times. I share with you my personal experience.

Tragedy struck my life when I suddenly and unexpectedly lost my mother. The pain and grief experienced was unimaginable, and it truly pushed me to the brink of despair. After this loss, my journey was further complicated by severe anxiety and battles with depression, including postpartum depression. These mental health challenges threatened to consume me, my family, and my career. Fortunately, this is when adapting my mindset WHILE surrounding myself with a wonderful network of supportive, loving, and resilient friends and family, made the difference and helped me bounce forward. This "support network" got me to where I am today. With the support of my loved ones and a strong determination to heal, I sought professional help and embarked on a journey of self-care and self-love. Part of this self-care journey was to tap into my internal "strengths". I discuss the importance of learning and understanding our strengths in my other books, "Yes I Can" and "An Empowered Life". These strengths empowered and unlocked a wellspring of resilience I didn't know existed. They helped me learn I can overcome anything, as long as I believe in myself and keep moving forward. I persevered. Perseverance is the fuel that propels us forward, even in the face of adversity. There have been many setbacks, failures, struggles I have overcome and many more ahead of me.

People often ask me, "how do you do it?" "...Just hearing your schedule and everything you do and accomplish, exhausts me". Being a wife and a mom of three, a female entrepreneur; starting and operating two businesses, a three-time best-selling author, supporting, developing events, and working to help over 40 nonprofits thrive every year, all while finding time for myself (work in progress), and fitting in a vacation now and again, how DO I do it?? I persevere. I am determined (mindset) to keep moving forward. Determination and perseverance to overcome obstacles, despite setbacks, have been instrumental in my personal and professional growth.

Most importantly, I could not and have not accomplished what I have on my own. I firmly and strongly believe that surrounding ourselves with positive, supportive individuals who believe in us will have a profound impact on our resilience. This strong support network of friends, family, mentors, and colleagues can greatly enhance our ability to bounce back from adversity.

Surrounding myself with positive and supportive people provided me with encouragement, guidance, and a sense of belonging. When we create and surround ourselves with a network of support that bolsters our resilience and inspires us, we can overcome any challenge. Who is in your network? Do you have what I like to call a "strength team"? Who supports and encourages your resiliency?

Finding and sharing vulnerability and authenticity

Yes, I know my strengths and find power, a superpower, in leveraging them to reach my goals and build success. Yes, I have overcome and found resiliency, bouncing back, from some of the deepest and darkest times in my life. However, resilience is not about putting on a facade of strength, but rather, having the courage to embrace vulnerability and authenticity.

As I mentioned earlier, it's not an everyday occurrence that I share or focus on my failures or setbacks with others. I do make a conscious effort to share, being vulnerable, with my support network and my strength team (my group of family, friends, colleagues who know of, fully support and encourage my strengths and challenges and I do the same). I will share with you, I pride myself in being genuine and authentic, as this is my ethical and moral compass. I am who I am and I will remain true to myself and my beliefs always. I never wish to present to someone, something I am not. I despise fake. I chose to surround myself with a support group, work environment and team of others who do the same. I encourage others to share their struggles and fears, thus creating a safe space for growth and resilience to flourish. Are you vulnerable with others?

Does your workplace promote resiliency? As a businesswoman and leader, I believe resilience in the workplace enables us to adapt to change, handle workplace stress, and navigate through setbacks. It is a priority of mine to foster resilience by promoting a positive work environment, provide and encourage opportunities for professional development (me included), and encourage open, honest communication.

Let me share a vulnerable moment with you. My everyday struggle and consistent challenge, affecting my own resilience, is self-care. I know that taking care of ourselves physically, emotionally, and mentally is crucial for building resilience. This is where I need the most growth. Everyone understands that engaging in activities that promote relaxation, regular exercise, healthy eating, and getting enough sleep all contribute to our overall well-being. However, do we make the time to put ourselves and our well-being first to take care of ourselves? I do not. This is a constant work in progress, reminding myself that self-care is not selfish, it is essential for maintaining resilience and preventing burnout.

My hope is that by sharing my journey, being vulnerable and authentic with you (and myself), will inspire you and others to stay strong, push through and work through your own challenges, and emerge stronger on the other side.

Practicing Gratitude and Appreciation

Gratitude is a powerful tool in nurturing resilience. By cultivating a mindset of gratitude, we shift our focus towards the positive aspects of our lives, fostering resilience and helping us navigate challenges with a sense of optimism and hope.

I am SO grateful for my life and all my accomplishments and blessings. This is something I try to share and say constantly. Again, not always perfect, and need to share more with others how grateful and thankful I am for their support, love, patience, and strength. One of my top five strengths is positivity. I have an internal way of looking for and finding positivity in situations.

Does this mean I am always positive, and nothing ever gets me down or feeling negative? Absolutely not. It just means I can more easily adapt in some situations to find and focus on optimism and hopefulness vs pessimism and despair.

Are you able to find positivity in the face of adversity? What do you do to express gratitude for those in your support network, friends, family, colleagues? For me, it's all about learning how I can make others feel special and valued. It's letting them know, as much as possible, how much they mean to me and how much I appreciate them. Always a work in progress.

If you have read this far in my chapter, I am so grateful for you. Time is the most special and precious gift anyone can give. You have given your time, a gift to me, to read and hear my vision and thoughts on resilience, and I thank you.

Conclusion

Resilience is not just about surviving; it is about thriving. When we cultivate resilience, we open ourselves up to a world of possibilities. Resilience helps us cope with stress, build healthier relationships, and achieve our goals. It enhances our overall well-being and allows us to embrace change and uncertainty with confidence.

Resilience is a powerful quality that can transform our lives. I can absolutely attest to this. Having and building resilience has allowed me to embrace challenges, bounce back from setbacks, and thrive in the face of adversity. Working daily to cultivate a growth mindset, build a strong support and "strength" network, striving to practice self-care, and setting realistic goals, I am consistently working to nurture resilience and unlock my full potential. My wish is that you too, will do the same. Resilience

A RESILIENT *Life*

is not about avoiding difficulties, but about developing the strength and courage to overcome them.

Please remember, YOU are capable of extraordinary resilience, and with it, you can conquer any obstacle that comes your way.

Sincerely and resiliently yours,

Vallye Adams

Vallye Adams

Etavele Solutions

Vallye Adams is the founder and CEO of Etavele Solutions, LLC, a national nonprofit consulting firm based in Tampa, Florida. Unique like her name, 'Etavele' ('elevate' spelled backwards) offers solutions to elevate and enhance events, engage boards, and specializes in proven sustainable revenue development in the not-for-profit sector.

Her "WOO" *(Winning Other's Over)*, communication and "includer" strengths, cultivate incredible relationships, sponsorships, and corporate partnerships. Vallye can connect the dots to elevate all areas, especially revenue and event fundraising. Vallye's ability to help customize, develop, and execute events, especially her trademarked, "C.A.M.P" (Community Ambassador Mission Program) has elevated client's revenue growth totaling over $10 million in the last 5 years. Experience in expansion throughout 22 states, Vallye focuses on grassroots efforts, building cohesive teams, motivating volunteers, and developing actively engaged structured boards.

Vallye's fun fact?? She offers to personally help your organization make "the ask" and show you the money $$! She is a **licensed female auctioneer (in multiple states) and professional master of ceremonies** with the incredible team at Alpert Enterprises! She travels anywhere and everywhere to not only consult and coach with everything your "nonprofit" needs, but also leads exceptional events (over 50 annually) using crowd loving, 'fun'draising techniques from the frontlines ...the stage!

Receiving the **2023 Female Nonprofit Consultant & Auctioneer of the Year (USA)** from *Acquisition International Magazine*, based in London, as well as a **#1 International Best-Selling Author of, "YES I CAN!" 16 Success Secrets from Inspiring Women around the world**, and collaborator of #1 National Best sellers,

"The Impact of Influence", and **"An Empowered Life",** Vallye is humbled and honored to share her success secrets and energy in print and on multiple podcasts, international publications, leadership series and conferences.

Vallye lives in Tampa. FL with her husband of 26 years and they have been blessed with three amazing children.

Email: vallye@etavelesolutions.com
Website: www.etavelesolutions.com
LinkedIn: vallyeadams or etavele-solutions

https://apnews.com/press-release/ein-presswire-newsmatics/philanthropy-tampa-e697d7b26b787bf6c27d7db0fcfb20b3

https://www.acquisition-international.com/issues/influential-businesswoman-awards-2023/56/

CHAPTER 5

Lisa Ohtaras

The Gift of Bouncing Forward

"Resilience highlights a person's strength of character; it is a process of successful adaptation to challenging life lessons and is a great gift to give to yourself." ~ Lisa Ohtaras

To The Divine World, The Light Beings Ascended Masters, and my Higher Self, I am eternally grateful for your education, guidance, unconditional love, support, spiritual acumen and gifts, and the Sacred work I have the privilege and honour to conduct.

I am grateful to my family, friends, affiliates, soul tribe, and clients who have assisted me on my spiritual journey. Thank you!

Lisa Ohtaras

Learning the art of resiliency and mastering the practice of being a highly resilient person is one of the greatest gifts a person can give to themselves and their loved ones.

Regardless of the privileged life one may be fortunate enough to be born into, life's lessons are consistently present. Lacking resiliency can make our life lessons difficult, painful, and depressive, and is frequently accompanied by health issues.

I have learned to master the art of resiliency since my spiritual awakening over two and a half decades ago when I was seriously health-challenged with Multiple Sclerosis (MS) warning signs, and I was able to heal myself without medications. Being resilient, adaptable to new situations, and able to bounce forward regardless of the often challenging, changing, and painful life lessons has been highly beneficial to me.

Consistent and committed inner work and spiritual growth combined with daily meditation were the keys to my self-healing. Over time, I was able to reverse my serious symptoms as my Soul acknowledged the inner work I was doing. My life changed when I discovered I was more than my physical body, and it continues to change as I continue along my spiritual journey and engage in inner work as part of my daily routine.

I am transforming generational trauma, emotional wounds and ancestral imprints, subsequently healing my Soul and expanding its consciousness.

It takes courage to do inner work and spiritual growth. The process of addressing old emotional wounds, hurts, and present time challenges and unpleasant experiences can be very painful. However, ignoring the emotional, physical, and spiritual wounds one is carrying will eventually lead to more pain, as it often results in health challenges, as was the case with me.

A RESILIENT *Life*

Why? Because your Soul is seeking the inner work and spiritual growth to be done.

I enjoy doing inner work and spiritual growth as I transform energy from within, my Inner Beings rejoice, and my Spirit (the physical entity part of me) heals and my Soul evolves.

Toxic, unpleasant, and challenging life situations when not addressed will eventually result in repeating patterns, depression, sadness, grief, feeling unfairness, fear, anxiety, hardship, health challenges and more.

When events transpire, it is done by design by your Soul in co-creation with a person, with others, or through situations, circumstances, and events.

Ask yourself, 'how does this make me feel?'

Where in your mind, body, and spiritual life are you feeling the effects of the situation? Are you experiencing pain (physical, emotional, mental), discomfort, severe fatigue, humiliation, depression, irritability, insomnia, fear, interference with your inner connection, and more?

Do you want to continue feeling like this?

What is the lesson or growth opportunity being presented to you by the universe and your Soul?

My life became a roller coaster when I discovered I was on planet Earth to assist people at a spiritual level. My emotions fluctuated with all the different experiences I was having.

I can say without hesitation that I have been a student at the School of Hard Knocks since I awakened from my spiritual slumber, when in 2003 I resigned from my much-loved nursing career and commenced working my Sacred Mission, my Soul's purpose.

My spiritual journey has had peaks and troughs, highs, and lows. The energy has been intermittent comprising a combination of harsh, turbulent, painful, emotional, and financially crippling times, isolating times, happy times, and some financially abundant times.

When I was married, I had it all. I had everything I wished for. However, when I walked away from my marriage, I walked away with heavy credit card debts. To this day I still have these debts. I live in a rental property, and I live a vastly different lifestyle to what I lived in my financially abundant years.

Financially challenging times have been a regular part of my daily life with intermittent periods of financially abundant days. I have the clarity and awareness to know that what I have been experiencing has been a combination of my karmic imprint, balancing past life karma, and Earth School lessons. I have achieved enormous growth relating to my past, current and post-divorce financial hardship. I'm grateful for the lessons which have helped

I see things and situations from a broader perspective than I had previously seen things. I have acquired awareness about the importance of inner work, and I know I must address the emotions and experiences as they play out and as they surface from within me. I have become extremely consciously aware of my own inadequacies, and addressing the energy of my personal shortcomings by doing the inner work which in turn restores my confidence. I have owned my mistakes and learned their lessons.

A RESILIENT *Life*

The Soul is recreating past timelines so we can 'feel it to heal it.' The Soul wants the healing of the experiences. The Higher Self rejoices whenever inner work and spiritual growth are done!

The daily growth I engage in is done so I have inner peace and balance. It is not done to change other people. I am clearly aware of spiritual laws, and I abide and honour them knowing everybody has free will. It is not my role to override free will in people and nor do I.

Energy healing, Soul healing, Soulful Forgiveness® work, coaching and hosting workshops have provided me with inconsistent income throughout the past 20 years. It has been a challenging journey! Fortunately, I have been blessed to have financial support whenever I required it, as the appropriate people were brought to me to loan me the money when I needed it. The universe is always looking out for me, and I am deeply grateful to all the people who have assisted me in my times of need.

In 2016, I was receiving daily phone calls from the banks after falling behind on my monthly credit card payments. I was in tears every day as I could not pay my bills because my income was insufficient. Due to my financial situation and the extenuating circumstances at that time, the banks kindly issued me with a moratorium (the temporary pause of my monthly repayments) to help ease the financial pressure. It was so humiliating and upsetting for me to be in that position! The practice of being resilient and the ability to bounce forward from being humiliated and angry with life in general, was an asset back then as it is today.

I learned great lessons during that challenging period of my life when I was facing harsh life-changing situations relating to wise money management and much more. Each time I pay a bill, particularly a credit card payment, I bless the payment I make with deep gratitude for being in the financial position to be able to do so.

In fact, since healing myself from my MS warning signs, I take nothing in my life for granted, not the air I breathe, my heartbeat, or the delicate balance of my body systems running without any effort and thought on my part. It is amazing how many things we take for granted until we no longer have access to them. I am in deep gratitude for everything in my life including the good, the unpleasant, the exceptionally good and the worst-case scenarios.

Being resilient and bouncing forward are ALWAYS my choices.

I consciously choose to see the growth opportunity with all challenging and unpleasant situations as they transpire. Being resilient and completing the inner work and spiritual growth are what help to keep me in balance. I recommend this to anyone seeking inner peace, clarity, improved health, and more.

During my day, I take the time each hour to ensure I clear my energy of any negative emotions that may have surfaced from within my subconscious mind, any external energy I may have absorbed from others, and I identify anything that has been said to me whether directly or indirectly that has triggered me. I ask myself '*how I have created this?*'

I sit in quiet with my eyes closed and ground myself by visualising roots coming out of the soles of my feet and going deep into Mother Earth. Then I take a deep inhalation into my lower abdominal area, pause for a few seconds, and exhale with

A RESILIENT *Life*

the intention of releasing any negative emotions or negative energy that is present or surfacing within my being.

Here is what I say:

Dear Higher Self,

I acknowledge the conscious thoughts surfacing from within me and the subconscious thoughts (from my Soul), or other energy that I have absorbed from other people or places, which are not for my highest and greatest good. I transmute the energy into light and love and return it across all time, all space, all dimensions, all realities, and all universes to Source to the place of origin where it originated. Thank you! Thank you! Thank you!

I am consistently releasing energy that no longer serves me and I protect my energy to minimise the absorption of other peoples' negative energy.

I am immediately aware when I have unpleasant energies or negative waves projected onto me. I simply do not feel good. Without any hesitation, I do the inner work and the spiritual growth to free myself of whatever is playing out, as it ALWAYS relates to spiritual growth. Everything is always being done for me and not to me.

Learning to be resilient and bouncing forward is an incredibly amazing gift a person can give to themselves. Sinking into waves of negative emotions can be minimized through the act of being resilient.

If a person does not address challenges as they happen, the suppressed energy implodes, and energy blockages are formed.

Denial has potentially harmful consequences to a person on the mental, emotional, physical, and spiritual levels. If the Soul observes the person is in denial relating to whatever is playing out, it recreates the situation and often amplifies the energy because the person is not addressing it. Hence people tend to become angry, bitter, resentful, agitated, humiliated, depressed, vindictive, unwell with aches and pains, manifest chronic illnesses, and other health challenges, have difficulty forgiving themselves and/or others, do not like themselves, and more.

The physical body is a powerful apparatus and temple when one learns to harness the energy contained within. All the answers you seek are within you.

This is why regardless of whatever is happening in my life, I consciously choose to address the situation as my Soul wants the energy transformed.

When we transition and return home to the non-physical spirit world, all material possessions are left behind. What is most significant for our Soul whilst we are living on planet Earth, is the amount of service we provide to assist humanity, the animal kingdom, Planet Earth – Gaia, or the spirit world, and the amount of growth we do to heal the Soul and expand the Soul's consciousness.

Although the people involved in whatever is transpiring that relates to me, quite often do not change, I change the way I perceive the situation. Emotions are amplified whenever one does the inner work, that is, the inner self is more peaceful relating to the situation that is addressed.

During my experiences throughout the past two and a half decades of doing inner work and spiritual growth, I have learned that doing inner work does not always prevent situations and circumstances from taking place.

A RESILIENT *Life*

Inner work and spiritual growth help heal the Soul's consciousness and the spirit (the physical entity part of you).

It is interesting to know that the experiences one has in relation to the growth the Soul is wanting is less turbulent than if a person does not do the growth.

I have repeatedly seen evidence of this. My Higher Self shows me and explains the before-growth energy and the energy following the growth. There is a positive transformation of energy that transpires! It is this transformation that leads to inner peace prevailing. The significance is the Inner Being(s) that created the situation to transpire are feeling more peaceful.

The more I do my inner work and spiritual growth the more resilient I become, and the more I realise the importance of this being done daily. Energy is constantly in motion. My Soul wants me to do the inner work and transform the energy being created internally and externally that relates to me and my well-being.

The answers to everything I need to know are with me! As they are within you also. Your Soul creates health issues, and your Soul can uncreate health issues, if it is for your highest good, as was the case with me 27 years ago. The health issues are present so we can do the inner work to help heal the Soul.

Discipline, perseverance, patience, commitment, and resilience are required when one does inner work and spiritual growth. It is well worth the time and energy one expends.

Emotional rewards are plentiful whenever you meditate in a quiet place, still your mind, tune into the depth of your inner self, and listen to the inner wisdom. Combining inner wisdom with spiritual growth helps a person to become resilient.

Lisa Ohtaras

The resiliency of one's being is a precious gift not just for the person but for their family, loved ones and affiliates. Bouncing forward having a clearer, broader perspective of situations, and being able to obtain solutions from within following unpleasant occurrences and experiences, raises a person's frequency, as opposed to functioning from a lower frequency or vibration.

Whenever you experience an unpleasant or painful experience, know you have what it takes within you to overcome the energy that has been created. The Soul would not allow it to happen if you could not cope with the energy being created.

Should you feel stagnant, blocked, have a heavy heart from emotional wounds, have challenges with forgiveness of yourself and others, or find yourself at a crossroads in your life and would like energy healing, intuitive guidance and implementable simplified solutions, I invite you to make contact with me via my Website at: www.caringenergetichealing.com.

My parting gift...

The following tips and wisdom have helped me to be resilient on my spiritual journey and Soul evolution and I hope they will be beneficial for you too...

1. Every morning and night protect your energy and cut cords from people, places, and anything else that are not for your greatest good.

2. Whenever you make mistakes, learn from the mistakes and be gentle with yourself and others. Mistakes are part of the Soul's journey.

3. Prior to going to sleep let go of any situation, person, people, or place that is causing you inner turmoil, or may have upset you

and your day. Here is an abbreviated version you can say, 'I let go of and forgive_____ (whomever you are not at peace with), and I forgive myself for whatever it is that transpired.' You will sleep better, and your Soul will be more peaceful.

4. Be the deliberate creator of your day! Plan it and visualise in your mind's eye how you want tomorrow or future days to transpire. You may want to script the details in writing and prior to going to sleep read it out aloud. Your Soul will then know exactly what you want and help you to accomplish it.

"Inner work, spiritual growth and energy healing are key components to the transformation of energy from within and helping the Soul's evolution." ~ Lisa Ohtaras

Thank you for reading my chapter.

Infinite blessings,

Lisa Ohtaras

Lisa Ohtaras

Caring Energetic Healing

Lisa Ohtaras has co-authored several Amazon Best Selling books, and is a renowned Energy Healer, Soul Healer, Intuitive Spiritual Coach, Spiritual Educator, Reiki Master, Seichim Master, Angelic Healing, Channel, Soulful Forgiveness® Practitioner & Workshop Facilitator, Thought Field Therapy Practitioner, and Compassion Key Practitioner.

Following Lisa's spiritual awakening from spiritual slumber over two and a half decades ago that was precipitated by her Multiple Sclerosis (MS) warning signs that she reversed without the use of any medication, Lisa has utilised her knowledge and gifts to help others in need.

Lisa conducts energetic healing and spiritual healing combined with her knowledge and experience relating to over 20 years of traditional medicine working as a registered nurse in a variety of fields, to go deeper than most forms of healing, to address the root cause and origin of the symptoms, ailments and problems being experienced.

Lisa helps with clarity, forgiveness of oneself and others, life purpose and more, resulting in the transformation of energy, improved health, greater awareness, higher energy levels and a deeper understanding of oneself.

Website: www.caringenergetichealing.com
Instagram: @lisaohtaras
LinkedIn: lisaohtaras

CHAPTER 6

Steph Gobraiel

The manual to business and motherhood called Life

A resilient life

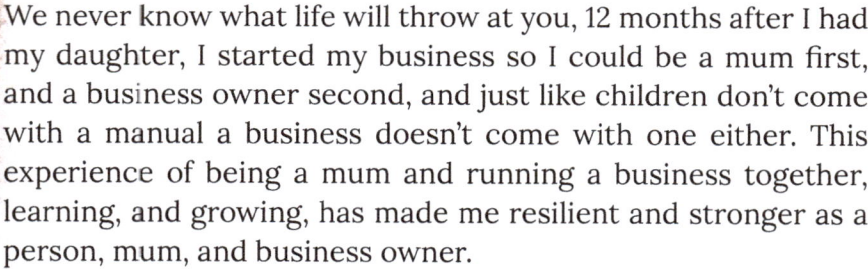

We never know what life will throw at you, 12 months after I had my daughter, I started my business so I could be a mum first, and a business owner second, and just like children don't come with a manual a business doesn't come with one either. This experience of being a mum and running a business together, learning, and growing, has made me resilient and stronger as a person, mum, and business owner.

It's been the largest self-growth journey in my life to date, I shared part of my earlier journey, especially around mum guilt in my first co-authored book called An Enlightened Life, and it's brought me to where we are in the present day.

I felt quite alone when I first started my business there was no family or friends who ran their own business to ask for advice or guidance from. Like anything new, I didn't know what to expect or what was going to come next. I think it's safe to say we all feel that at some stage of the business journey. Being in business for four-plus years has taught me tough but valuable lessons.

Part of being a business owner is an ongoing self-growth journey, not just for your business journey but to grow as a person, It takes time, and it means coming out of your comfort zone and working on the mindset to get past the hurdles in order to grow and move forward. It's all part of the journey. It's not an easy thing to do but when you take it one step at a time anything is achievable.

From mum guilt to resilience

There is no manual when you have a child and starting a business is the same because it brings in your personality and experience which is only unique to us. In my previous co-authored book, I spoke about how mum guilt consumed me in the first few years of my daughter's life, to the degree that I couldn't drive off after dropping her at daycare, shaking and waiting for time to pass to be able to call them and know that she's settled before I can pull myself together and leave.

Was it because I had no family support which meant my daughter wasn't used to being around other people looking after her and when mum left her, her world would shatter? How do you change something that you don't have control over? You can't and it's not something anyone can just understand unless you are in the same situation.

A RESILIENT *Life*

It was an educator who noticed how much it affected me at drop-off because of my screaming child and she had a chat with me about finding ways to cope because in her own words "it's not healthy for me to go on like this." That was the moment in time when I realised and noticed how much it was affecting me.

I then started implementing strategies such as breathing and counting, to help me cope, and being conscious of how I was feeling was the beginning of that change in my life. Being mindful is powerful and helps you get through what's happening no matter how hard the situation may be on you.

As time went on, I learned that it was doing more damage, mentally than good, so I learned to acknowledge it, reassure myself, and then find a way forward to get on with my day. It's taken me time, practice, and self-love to reach this point. Does it still happen? absolutely because as a mum it never goes away but there is a positive way, I can live with it. We can only do our best at the end of the day. It feels like it's a taboo topic we don't talk about enough and there shouldn't be any shame when it comes from a place of love.

There are different ways of learning resilience in business and it's the tough lessons that forge the path ahead.

Learning the lessons of having boundaries and being in alignment with values

One of my core values in business and personal life is family. When I started my business, I was working around the clock to build up my business. I very quickly realised I was working like an employee, and to what end?

As a business owner, I'm supposed to set my hours and create the business I want to work around my family not the other way around. Right?

I was working with a client who did not have children and it was difficult for him to understand how I was juggling the two (business and a sick daughter) at the same time. I had a client meeting and explained at the beginning my daughter was sick and that we might be interrupted for that reason, but the more we got interrupted I could see the frustration on his face, and he clearly didn't understand I had to look after my very young and sick daughter at the time while we had the meeting. This put a lot of pressure and stress on me and it only made me feel anxious.

I realised in that moment I didn't want to work with people like that because I shouldn't be made to feel any less because I was trying to look after my sick daughter, in hindsight I should have postponed the meeting but it was an eye opener for me.

What are your values in business and are you practicing them?

When I came up for air and was able to take a step back, I added the family to my values because as the primary carer, I'm doing the heavy lifting for my daughter. What I did to make this change, wasn't only to add it to my values but communicate to potential clients in my discovery calls (initial conversation) my situation and If it was an issue, it wouldn't be a good fit for me. By having that boundary, it sifted through the clients I didn't want to work with quite quickly without wasting anyone's time. This is one of the examples I learned how to ensure that my boundaries were being met and also stepping up and owning my own highest value - family.

A RESILIENT *Life*

Even when I'm sick, especially in autumn and winter I try to push through but we're all human and sometimes you just need to rest to recover. Communicating with clients that I'm sick and I'll be offline for a few days isn't going to make the world stop.

This is giving myself the permission to put myself first so I can recover, be a mum then a business owner. We need to give ourselves permission to rest and recover especially when our bodies are telling us to. Do you have boundaries in place that you honour?

This ties into integrity (another value of mine) it is a two-way street in business and respect and communication are important, if it's lacking one or the other then there is already a problem that needs to be addressed. This comes over time in business but not every client is going to be an ideal client for our business and that's OK. There are plenty of clients that will be aligned with your values and what you have to offer. It's a matter of finding and attracting them through standing strong on your values and beliefs.

Low times in business are crucial lessons

All businesses go through busy and not-so-busy times. My ultimate lesson in business was in the span of three months most of my clients finished up with me and as happy as I was for them, that they were able to move forward, my business took a hit. The biggest in all my years in business. It made me extremely nervous but I kept telling myself "There are reasons why and I need to ride it out".

Also, at the time I realised, I was heavily relying on referral work and that I wasn't doing a lot of networking and really getting my business out there to be heard and seen.

I was in a comfortable place and didn't really think there was a need to get out there but that's the thing with owning a business, you can never do enough to get your business out there and to expect the unexpected. I was lucky to have had savings to keep things ticking over but that's not a money tree.

That's when I started working on my business but by that point, it was too late for the current year, as I always tell my clients things don't come to fruition in business overnight everything takes time. The new year came around and that's when I focused on the grandfather of awards (which I became a finalist for) and wrote my first co-authored book.

February rolled around and I decided to try a few new things and like the light of a switch, it was back to business. What were those testing months trying to teach me? Not to have all my eggs in one basket and the importance of continually working on my business even when business is thriving. It's a few hard lessons to learn, but if there is going to be survival then we need to learn to adapt and pay attention to signs around us. Even when you're the hamster on the wheel because there are always warning signs.

The lessons learned

Like being a mum, business is a constant state of learning and lessons to be learned. It's the unknown we must go through to come out on the other side stronger and through self-growth. No matter how you learn resilience in business it needs to be learned in order to keep your business going.

This goes hand in hand with boundaries and values, we need to be resilient in order to have boundaries and they can come from our values because I want clients who share the same values as I do in business in order to be on the same page.

We can't deny that business is like a rollercoaster even more so in tough economic times. It's important to keep re-assessing what's working and what isn't in business. Yes, absolutely clients are what pay the bills but if you don't have a strategy for your business how will new clients find you?

Just like the lessons learned, it has then allowed me to step into my power as a mum and business owner.

Forward: As an Online Business manager this is how I help set my clients up for success.

I'd love for you to reflect on your business and ask yourself these questions that come up when I'm speaking to potential clients –

- Are you taking a holistic approach to business? (Business and personal)
- Is your business running you or are you running your business?
- Are you willing to step out of your comfort zone in order to grow your business?
- What is holding you back from taking that next step forward in business?
- Are you honouring your values and boundaries at the moment?
- Does your business make you feel empowered? (Some sort of balance between work and life)

Redefining Empowerment

The definition of having a business is like having a child or a fur baby, you're constantly thinking about how to nourish, love, and grow it.

As a mum who started motherhood and a business thinking "I can do it all" (to the degree my first logo had a superhero cape), I couldn't.

Pre-baby it was easier because even if I worked extremely long days, I had the nights and weekends to look after myself. It's very different when you have a child and ask, "Where is this village?" It's more like 'What village?'

A major lesson that's been learned on this rollercoaster called motherhood and business is that we don't have to do it all. As women, we should be able to pick and choose what we want to do. Who are you trying to prove yourself to? The only person you should be trying to prove yourself to is you. No one else cares. None of it matters if your health is going to pay the price like mine did.

The only question that needs to be asked is 'What do you need to do to empower yourself first? That's what matters at the end of the day.

Book a complimentary clarity call and get ready for actionable insights that will move you and your business forward. This is valued at $110.

Steph Gobraiel

Steph Gobraiel is a highly experienced online business manager and founder of S38 Business Management. As a former executive assistant to high-level corporate managers, she has a wealth of experience and business knowledge. Steph has worked with big corporates such as Westpac, CPA Australia and Intel, and holds a Diploma in Business Administration and Management.

As an OBM, Steph takes a holestic approach to business and personal and helps small business owners create effective habits to run their businesses more efficiently. Her sound advice streamlines business operations and Steph specialises in helping her clients build impressive online profiles.

Steph is dedicated to supporting women in business and is a Host for Women's Networking events. She believes seeking business support is a sign of strength and growth. With practical support and the right mix of empathy, wisdom and accountability, Steph helps service-based businesses untangle their business knots and create a sustainable plan for the future.

With a passion for helping owners build their businesses around their families, Steph helps overwhelmed entrepreneurs say goodbye to exhaustion and hello to a successful business (that doesn't take over every moment of their lives).

Steph was a finalist for Ausmumpreneur (Professional Services of the year category) 2023 Local Business Awards in Business Services, Australian Ladies In Business Awards (Online Business of the year category) and Business Xcellence Awards 2023.

With her depth of experience and expertise, Steph is a trusted adviser in helping her clients achieve their goals and reach their full potential. And as a dynamic and driven individual, she is a valuable virtual team member for the modern small business.

Website: https://s38businessmanagement.com.au/
Facebook: @s38businessmanagement
Instagram: @steph_gobraiel.obm
LinkedIn: www.linkedin.com/in/stephanie-gobraiel
An Enlightened Life – Part 1 - https://bit.ly/3QvevNp
Take the Business health check here - https://bit.ly/3rLMu9V

CHAPTER 7

Kleo Merrick

Resilient Entrepreneurship

How to Live a Strong and Successful Life

"If you can't fly then run, if you can't run then walk, if you can't walk then crawl, but whatever you do you have to keep moving forward" ~ Martin Luther King Jr

As entrepreneurs, we know that building a successful business is not a walk in the park. It takes hard work, dedication, and a whole lot of resilience. Resilience is the ability to bounce back from setbacks, adapt to change, and keep moving forward in the face of adversity. It's a crucial quality for any entrepreneur to have, especially in today's fast-paced and ever-changing business landscape.

In this chapter, we will explore how to live a resilient life as an entrepreneur. We will discuss the importance of resilience in entrepreneurship, how to cultivate a resilient mindset and the role of experience and knowledge in building resilience. We will also cover topics such as overcoming failure and setbacks, planning and organization for resilience, leveraging support and mentorship, harnessing technology and innovation, and financial resilience in entrepreneurship. Finally, we will explore how to build resilience in new ventures and how to stay resilient during the Covid-19 pandemic.

Key Takeaways

- Resilience is a crucial quality for any entrepreneur to have in today's fast-paced and ever-changing business landscape.

- Cultivating a resilient mindset, leveraging support and mentorship, and harnessing technology and innovation are all important strategies for building resilience as an entrepreneur.

- Overcoming failure and setbacks, planning and organization, and financial resilience are also key components of a resilient life as an entrepreneur.

A RESILIENT *Life*

Understanding Resilience in Entrepreneurship

As entrepreneurs, we face numerous challenges and obstacles every day. These challenges can be in the form of negative events, setbacks, or unexpected obstacles that can shake our confidence and make us question our abilities. However, to succeed in entrepreneurship, we need to develop a resilient mindset that allows us to bounce back from these challenges.

Resilience is the ability to adapt, recover quickly from adversity and keep moving forward in the face of setbacks and challenges. Resilience is not something that we're born with; it's a skill that we can develop over time.

Resilient entrepreneurs are those who have developed a mindset that allows them to bounce back from adversity. They see setbacks as opportunities to learn and grow, rather than as failures. They understand that failure is an essential part of the entrepreneurial journey and that it's not something to be feared.

To develop a resilient mindset, we need to focus on building our emotional and mental resilience. This means developing the ability to manage our emotions, stay positive, and maintain a sense of perspective when faced with challenges.

We can build emotional and mental resilience by:

- Practising mindfulness and meditation to help manage stress and anxiety

- Developing a growth mindset that emphasises learning and growth over fixed abilities

- Building a support network of mentors, peers, and friends who can provide support and guidance when we need it

- Developing a sense of purpose and meaning in our work which can help us stay motivated and focused during challenging times

In summary, resilience is a critical skill for entrepreneurs. It's the ability to bounce back from setbacks and challenges and keep moving forward towards our goals. By developing a resilient mindset and building our emotional and mental resilience, we can overcome obstacles and achieve success in our entrepreneurial journey.

Cultivating a Resilient Mindset

As entrepreneurs, we face many challenges and setbacks on a daily basis. To live a resilient life, we need to cultivate a resilient mindset. But how? We must focus on our:

Confidence

We need to believe in ourselves and our abilities, even when things get tough. This means focusing on our strengths and accomplishments and using them to overcome challenges.

Passion

When we are passionate about what we do, we are more likely to persevere through difficult times. We need to remind ourselves of why we started our businesses in the first place and use that passion to fuel our resilience.

Grit

We need to be willing to put in the hard work and effort required to overcome obstacles. This means pushing ourselves beyond our comfort zones and embracing discomfort as a necessary part of growth.

Behaviours

We need to develop positive habits and routines that support our mental and emotional well-being. This might include regular exercise, meditation, or journaling.

Positive adaptation

We need to be able to adapt to changing circumstances and find new ways of doing things when old methods are no longer effective. This means being open to new ideas and perspectives and embracing change as an opportunity for growth.

Uncertainty

This is a fact of life for entrepreneurs, and developing a resilient mindset means learning to embrace it. We need to be comfortable with the unknown and be willing to take risks in order to achieve our goals.

Positive Emotions

We need to focus on the good things in our lives and find joy and gratitude in the present moment. This means practising mindfulness and being fully present in the here and now.

By cultivating a resilient mindset, we can overcome the challenges and setbacks that come with being an entrepreneur. We can bounce back from adversity, adapt to change, and remain positive in the face of uncertainty.

The Role of Experience and Knowledge

Experience and knowledge are crucial to success as our experiences shape us and teach us valuable lessons that we can use to navigate challenges and overcome obstacles.

Education & Learning

What new knowledge and skills are you seeking to stay ahead of the curve and adapt to changing circumstances? Whether it's attending conferences, taking courses, or reading books, there is always something new to learn.

Embracing Failure

Failure is not a reflection of our worth or abilities, but rather an opportunity to learn and grow. By reviewing our failures and reflecting on what we could have done differently, we can develop a better understanding of ourselves and our businesses.

Seeking Support

Surround ourselves with supportive people who can provide guidance and encouragement. We should seek out mentors, advisors, and peers who can offer different perspectives and help us stay focused on our goals.

A RESILIENT *Life*

Experience and knowledge are essential components of building resilience as an entrepreneur, by continually learning and growing, embracing failure and surrounding ourselves with supportive people, we can develop the mental tools we need to overcome challenges and succeed in our businesses.

Overcoming Failure and Setbacks

As entrepreneurs, we know that failure and setbacks are inevitable. However, it's how we respond to these challenges that defines our success. Here are some tips to help us overcome failure and bounce back stronger:

- **Acknowledge and accept the failure**: It's important to acknowledge and accept the failure or setback. Denying or ignoring it will only prolong the process of moving forward. Accepting it allows us to learn from our mistakes and take action to prevent similar situations in the future.

- **Reflect and learn from the experience**: Take time to reflect on the situation and identify what went wrong. Ask ourselves what we could have done differently and what we can learn from the experience. This will help us avoid making the same mistakes in the future.

- **Stay positive and focus on the future**: It's easy to get caught up in negative thoughts and feelings after a failure or setback. However, it's important to stay positive and focus on the future. We must remind ourselves of our strengths and the progress we have made so far. This will help us stay motivated and continue moving forward.

- **Adapt and adjust our approach**: Failure and setbacks provide an opportunity to adapt and adjust our approach.

We must be willing to try new things and take calculated risks. This will help us stay ahead of the curve and be better prepared for future challenges.

- **Seek support and guidance:** It's important to seek support and guidance from others. This can be from a mentor, coach, or even a friend or family member. They can provide valuable insights and advice to help us overcome the challenge.

Remember, failure and setbacks are a natural part of the entrepreneurial journey. It's how we respond to these challenges that will define our success.

Planning and Organisation for Resilience

As entrepreneurs, we know that planning and organisation are key to success. But did you know that they are also essential for building resilience?

A Clear Vision

This means having a long-term goal or mission statement that guides our decisions and actions. By having a clear vision, we can stay focused on what is truly important and avoid getting side-tracked by short-term obstacles.

Realistic Plans

Setting achievable goals and breaking them down into smaller, manageable tasks. By taking small steps towards our goals, we can build momentum and stay motivated, even in the face of setbacks.

Preparedness

This means anticipating potential challenges and having contingency plans in place. For example, we might have a backup supplier in case our primary supplier falls through, or we might have a rainy-day fund to help us weather unexpected financial challenges.

Organisation

By keeping our workspace and digital files organised, we can reduce stress and avoid wasting time searching for important documents or information. This can also help us stay focused and productive, even when we are dealing with unexpected challenges.

Leveraging Support and Mentorship

As entrepreneurs, we often face challenges that can be overwhelming and stressful. To live a resilient life, it's essential to have a support network and mentors who can guide us through difficult times.

Having a support network of family, friends, and colleagues can provide us with emotional support and encouragement. They can help us stay positive and motivated, even when things get tough. It's important to surround ourselves with people who believe in us and our vision.

Mentors can also play a crucial role in our entrepreneurial journey. They can provide us with guidance and advice based on their own experiences. Finding a mentor who has been through similar challenges can be invaluable. They can help us avoid common pitfalls and provide us with a fresh perspective on our business.

When looking for a mentor, it's important to choose someone who is a good fit for our personality and business goals. We should look for someone who is willing to invest their time and energy into our success. A mentor who is approachable and easy to talk to can make all the difference.

In addition to finding a mentor, we can also leverage support networks such as business associations, networking groups, and online communities. These groups can provide us with access to resources, knowledge, and connections that can help us grow our business.

Leveraging support and mentorship is essential for living a resilient life as an entrepreneur. Having a support network and mentors can provide us with the emotional support, guidance, and resources we need to overcome challenges and achieve our goals.

Harnessing Technology and Innovation

As entrepreneurs, we know that technology and innovation are constantly evolving and shaping the way we live our lives. We need to harness these tools to build resilience in our businesses and personal lives. Here are some ways we can do that:

Embrace Apps and Technology

Apps and technology have made it easier than ever to stay organised, manage our time, and communicate with others. We can use apps like Trello or Asana to manage our tasks and projects, and tools like Slack or Zoom to communicate with our teams and clients. By embracing these tools, we can work more efficiently and stay connected even when we're not in the same room.

Stay Ahead of the Curve

Innovation is key to staying ahead of the competition. We need to be constantly looking for new ways to improve our products or services and to innovate in our industry. Keeping up with the latest trends and technologies can help us identify new opportunities and stay ahead of the curve.

Learn from the Best

We can learn a lot from successful innovators like Apple and Intel. By studying their products and strategies, we can gain insights into what makes a successful business and how to stay ahead of the curve. We can also attend conferences and events to learn from experts in our industry and stay up to date with the latest trends.

Be Open to Change

Innovation and technology are constantly changing, and we need to be open to change as well. We need to be willing to pivot our business strategies and adapt to new technologies and trends. By being open to change, we can stay ahead of the curve and build resilience in our businesses.

By embracing apps and technology, staying ahead of the curve, learning from successful innovators, and being open to change, we can build businesses that are resilient and adaptable to change.

Financial Resilience in Entrepreneurship

When it comes to building a resilient life as an entrepreneur, financial resilience is a crucial aspect. As entrepreneurs, we need to be financially prepared to face any challenges that come our way. Here are some tips on how to build financial resilience in entrepreneurship:

1. Capital

Capital is the lifeblood of any business. Without adequate capital, it's difficult to get a business off the ground, let alone sustain it. As entrepreneurs, we need to be financially savvy and ensure that we have enough capital to cover our expenses, invest in growth, and weather any financial storms that may come our way.

To build financial resilience in entrepreneurship, we need to be strategic in our capital planning. We should create a budget, forecast our cash flow, and have a contingency plan in case of unexpected expenses or downturns in the market. We should also explore different sources of capital, such as loans, grants, and equity investments, to ensure that we have access to the funds we need to grow and thrive.

2. Financial Resources

We need to have access to other financial resources to build resilience in entrepreneurship. This includes having a good credit score, building a strong network of investors and advisors, and staying up to date on financial trends and regulations.

Consider investing in insurance policies, such as liability insurance, professional indemnity, property insurance, and business interruption insurance, to protect ourselves against unexpected events that could impact our business. By having these financial resources in place, we can build a strong foundation for our business and ensure that we're prepared for any financial challenges that may come our way.

3. Financial Planning

Finally, we need to have a clear understanding of our financial goals, both short-term and long-term, and create a plan to achieve them.

This includes setting realistic financial targets, tracking our expenses and revenue, and making adjustments as needed. We should also work with financial advisors and accountants to ensure that we're making informed financial decisions and taking advantage of any tax breaks or incentives that may be available to us.

In conclusion, building financial resilience in entrepreneurship is essential for long-term success. By being strategic in our capital planning, having access to financial resources, and engaging in financial planning, we can ensure that we're prepared for any financial challenges that may come our way.

Building Resilience in New Ventures

Starting a business can be an exciting and rewarding experience, but it can also be challenging and stressful. As entrepreneurs, we must learn to build resilience in our new ventures to ensure their survival and success. Here are some ways we can do that:

1. Develop a Strong Business Model

Take the time to develop a well-thought-out plan that includes a clear mission statement, market analysis, and financial projections. By having a solid plan in place, we can better navigate the inevitable challenges that will arise.

2. Embrace Failure as a Learning Opportunity

As discussed earlier in the chapter, starting a new venture involves taking risks, and not all of them will pay off. When we experience failure, it's important to view it as a learning opportunity rather than a setback. By reflecting on our mistakes and identifying what we can do differently next time, we can become more resilient and better equipped to handle future challenges.

3. Surround Ourselves with Supportive People

Entrepreneurship can be a lonely journey, but it doesn't have to be. By surrounding ourselves with supportive people, such as mentors, advisors, and fellow entrepreneurs, we can build a strong network that can offer guidance, feedback, and encouragement when we need it most.

4. Prioritize Self-Care

Running a new venture can be all-consuming, but it's essential that we prioritize self-care to avoid burnout. This includes taking breaks, getting enough sleep, eating well, and engaging in activities that bring us joy and relaxation. By taking care of ourselves, we can better handle the stress and uncertainty that comes with entrepreneurship.

A RESILIENT *Life*

5. Stay Agile and Adaptable

In today's fast-paced business environment, it's essential that we stay agile and adaptable. By being open to change and willing to pivot, when necessary, we can better respond to market shifts and emerging trends. This flexibility is key to the survival and success of any new venture.

By following these tips, we can build resilience in our new ventures and increase our chances of success. Remember, starting a business is a journey, and it's important to celebrate our wins along the way.

Conclusion

Living a resilient life as an entrepreneur is crucial for our growth, progress, and success. It allows us to overcome challenges and setbacks and emerge even stronger. By developing our resilience, we can improve our performance and well-being, and achieve our desired outcomes.

To live a resilient life, we must cultivate a growth mindset, practice self-care, and build a support network. We should also learn from our failures and setbacks and use them as opportunities to grow and improve. By staying positive and focusing on our strengths, we can overcome obstacles and achieve our goals.

It's important to remember that resilience is not a fixed trait, but a skill that can be developed over time. By taking small steps every day, we can build our resilience and become more adaptable, flexible, and resourceful. With practice and perseverance, we can live a more resilient life as entrepreneurs and achieve our full potential.

Kleo Merrick

Kleo Merrick

Merrick Courses Pty Ltd

Kleo Merrick is a 4-time Amazon #1 International Bestselling Author, Speaker, and Freelance Content & Marketing Strategist.

Kleo is the CEO of Merrick Courses, a company she founded in 2013 where she runs successful Workshops, Online Training Programs and teaches businesses how to market their services with Sales Funnels, Webinars and Online Courses. And educates them on how to manoeuvre Digital Marketing specifically for Entrepreneurs.

Her clients say: "Kleo taught me more in 2 hours than it would have taken me 5 years to learn myself…!!!" – Cathy Kingsley

She is the author of:

~ 'An Empowered Life: 10 Inspirational Stories From Women Around the World Who Have Dared to Live and Empowered Life',

~ 'An Inspired Life: 10 Inspirational Stories From Women Around the World Who Have Dared to Follow Their Passion',

~ 'I Did It: 16 Mindset Secrets To Transform The Life You Have Into The Ultimate Life you Desire',

~ 'Yes, I Can: 16 Success Secrets Form Inspiring Women Around The World', and

~ 'Compelling Selling: How To Earn More By Selling Less'.

Kleo is extremely passionate about Creating a Community of Passionate Business Owners and Upskilling them in the Digital World.

Email: kleo@kleomerrick.com
Facebook: www.facebook.com/marketingwithkleo/
Instagram: www.instagram.com/kleomerrick/
LinkedIn: www.linkedin.com/in/kleomerrick/
Website: www.kleomerrick.com

www.ingramcontent.com/pod-product-compliance
Lightning Source LLC
Chambersburg PA
CBHW041319110526
44591CB00021B/2836